The Inclusive God

Steven Shakespeare is the Anglican chaplain at Liverpool Hope University and teaches in the Department of Theology and Religious Studies. He is the author of *Kierkegaard, Language and the Reality of God*.

Hugh Rayment-Pickard is an Anglican priest working in West London, a regular columnist on the *Church Times* and the author of numerous scholarly and popular books including *The Devil's Account*, a study of Philip Pullman's treatment of Christianity.

The Inclusive God

Reclaiming Theology for an Inclusive Church

Steven Shakespeare
and
Hugh Rayment-Pickard

CANTERBURY
PRESS
Norwich

© Steven Shakespeare and Hugh Rayment-Pickard 2006
First published in 2006 by the Canterbury Press Norwich
(a publishing imprint of Hymns Ancient & Modern Limited,
a registered charity)
9–17 St Alban's Place, London
N1 0NX

www.scm-canterburypress.co.uk

British Library Cataloguing in Publication data

A catalogue record for this book is available
from the British Library

ISBN 1-85311-741-2/978-1-85311-741-1

Typeset by Regent Typesetting, London
Printed and bound in Great Britain by
William Clowes Ltd, Beccles, Suffolk

Contents

Acknowledgements

The authors would like to thank the following who at various times read and offered valuable comments on the text: Ann Alexander, Sally Bower, Rachel Carr, Mary Clarke, Mike Deed, Alan Everett, Matt Thompson, and Andrew Willson.

Foreword

The Village

It all happened such a long time ago, yet it's still so very difficult to bear talking about. This village has been burdened with a dark and guilty secret. We all knew about it. We were all a part of it, one way or another. But we've never properly spoken about it since. It's a conversation that has never happened.

Back then, it was such a traumatic time in our history, a time of huge fear and instability. You have to understand, at that time the very existence of the village was at stake. People feared for their lives and for the lives of their children. There were no police here, and the rule of law has never really operated. So yes, we have lived one great big lie. But we had to sort things out somehow. And now, of course, now we have been found out.

It all began with a fight. It usually does. Two families fell out over some stupid insult – though no one can really remember what it was about any more. Probably something to do with money or sex. One family started having a go, the other replied with more of the same. Soon they were throwing insults and punches. And then there was a stabbing. Remember, we don't have a police force. As things went on more and more people started to get drawn into the fight. The violence grew, people started to be killed. It was like a fire that was out of control. We all feared for our children.

And then it happened. It was confusing at first. She was this

weird girl who used to hang around on the edge of the village, sing-
ing to herself. Nobody ever took much notice of her, except the
kids who would call her all the rude names they learnt in the play-
ground. She was a real oddball for sure, but she didn't deserve what
happened.

I remember it was a Friday, because that's the day I go into the
village to do some shopping. And that's when I saw her. She was
slung on the back of a cart, her face all smashed up, her clothes
ripped, her body covered with blood and bruises. It was disgusting
what those bastards did to her. We'll probably never know exactly
who did it. But right there next to her, the brothers from the two
families sat with each other drinking beer. Drinking a bloody beer.
And from that time on, the fight between the two families was over.

Throughout the village there was so much relief that the whole
thing was over, we all tried to forget about the girl. The cart took
her away and dumped her on the other side of the river. The two
families were all forced smiles and backslapping. And then some
story started doing the rounds that the fight was some huge mis-
understanding and that it was really the girl's fault all along. It was
sick really, but we didn't care. We were safe. Even the priest was
happy. He had been in the village when she was carted away. He
gave her the last rites and made the whole thing seem OK. I mean,
if the priest is on board, what can the rest of us say?

In his sermons, the priest talked a lot about sacrifice. A sacrifice
would save us, he would always say. No wonder his church stank
like an abattoir. And now it was almost as if the girl was a sacri-
fice for the village. With her gone, we were all going to be fine. As
someone called Caiaphas once said: 'You do not understand that it
is better for one person to die for the people than to have the whole
village destroyed.' The priest even claimed that all the trouble in
the village must have been the girl's fault because everything was
fine after she went away.

And here's another thing we are not supposed to say. The girl wasn't the only one who disappeared like this. It happened quite a lot. Whenever there was trouble, it was always some weirdo that was to blame. Last year there was this boy who liked other boys. He ended up in a ditch. Then, before that, there was this old man who used to get confused. In fact, anybody who was a bit different – they were the ones that would end up in the ditch. And we would never say anything, because when they died we were safe. We have lived like this for years.

Sure there were a few people who came and said the whole thing was wrong. God wants mercy, not sacrifice, said Hosea. More radical still, the poet Isaiah started singing about the weirdoes as if they were important. He called them 'despised and rejected by men'; 'as one from whom men hide their faces he was despised, and we esteemed him not. Surely he has borne our grief and carried our sorrows; yet we esteemed him stricken, smitten by God, and afflicted. But he was wounded for our transgressions, he was bruised for our iniquities; upon him was the chastisement that made us whole, and with his stripes we are healed.' It was radical stuff.

Then one day this man came into the village and, somehow, he saw our guilty secret almost at once. He just looked at you and you knew that he knew. He was kind enough, but just looking at him made us all feel guilty. The priest hated him the most and they would row all the time. The stranger liked to quote from books written by Hosea and Isaiah. One day he sent the priest apoplectic by comparing him to a whitewashed tomb that looks beautiful on the outside but inside is full of the bones of the dead. But he was completely right. We all knew it, but we just couldn't face it. And then he started to name all the people who had been killed – 'from the blood of the righteous Abel to the blood of Zechariah, whom you murdered between the sanctuary and the altar'. Again the priest went ballistic.

He was an extraordinary man. People really took to him. In him the great lie was over. People would come out in the evenings to hear him speak. It was a wonderful and scary message, like a weight had been lifted from our shoulders. 'You know all these people you have killed,' he would say, 'I'm on their side. I am one of them. In as much as you do it to them, you do it to me.' He turned everything upside down. He was on the side of the girl who used to sing to herself, the boy who liked boys and the old man. The street kids called him good news.

But nobody likes to be shamed by the truth and he made lots of enemies. And right at the top of the list were the religious people. All those pious frauds that go to church and sing hymns: they still won't talk about the girl, they still won't admit what's been going on around here for years.

And so now this wonderful stranger also lies dead in a ditch. He told the truth and they strung him up for it. I want to be physically sick. As those thugs started on him, we all reverted to our gutless past. We did nothing. I ran away scared. I don't have his courage or his appetite for truth. I have kids, remember. Please God help us. Do something. Or things might never change around here. We need a miracle.

Inclusive Church

This book is intended to make one thing absolutely clear. Inclusivity is not an optional extra for Christians, it has nothing to do with being liberal, it's not a churchy version of political correctness. It's a gospel imperative, fundamental to the nature of God and at the very heart of the mission and ministry of our Lord Jesus Christ. It's orthodox Christianity. Inclusivity is often about homosexuality because the persecution of homosexuals, like the persecution of the Jews, is a litmus test for the presence of fascism, theological or otherwise.

Jesus comes into the village to stand alongside the despised and rejected. Either we stand with him, or we stand with the pious Caiaphas who cynically argued that the despised outsider is acceptable collateral damage in the overall story of salvation. If that's your salvation story, then you can never be on Jesus' side – for Jesus turns himself into the despised outsider and is subsequently lynched by the faithful. It's a pattern that just keeps on repeating itself.

Giles Fraser
Putney, April 2006

Introduction

Finding Our Voice

The Church should be inclusive because God is inclusive. Bluntly stated, that is the claim made by this book. We will try to give our reasons for this claim, and we will seek to do justice to the ambiguity and depth of real life. We are not interested in unexamined dogma. We do not believe in 'answers' to life's questions which filter out all the struggles, doubts and unknowing which are at the heart of human experience. But nor are we concerned with being 'relevant' for its own sake. The only justification for building an inclusive Church is that *this is what reality demands of us*. Inclusion is truth.

This book will flesh out what inclusion means by looking at what matters most in Christian theology: creation, revelation, Jesus' life, death and resurrection, the Church. It will end with an exploration of the nature of God. Our claim throughout will be that Christianity is inclusive to its core.

At a minimum, and at an administrative level, this means that the Church should no longer exclude from its life and ministry those who fall foul of merely cultural prejudices. For St Paul, inclusive theology and ecclesiology were focused on the status of gentiles, slaves and women. The inclusion issues of our day concern the participation of lesbians and gay men, women and black people. However, inclusive theology is not simply about the Church and its organizational policies at any particular juncture in history. It is about the world we share, the life we lead in common with all humanity. Inclusive theology is a joyful, outward-facing declaration that we are made and fulfilled by the love of God fleshed out in Christ, and spread abroad by the Spirit. It is a life-changing love which challenges every limitation we place on our ties of solidarity and responsibility. God makes all, draws all, saves all. Inclusive Christianity has for so long been at the heart of Christian service, peacemaking, action for justice and simple everyday kindness. Today, it is once more finding its radical, missionary, unapologetic voice. Today, it is reclaiming the mainstream of theology.

These might seem absurdly exaggerated, even self-contradictory, statements to make. How can a theology which emphasizes openness and reticence justify such grand and absolute claims? There is an echo here of a familiar charge laid against theological liberals: that their tolerance is merely a mask for Western, Enlightenment, prejudices, the arrogance with which they seek to dismiss all other voices and forms of rationality but their own. A kind of 'liberal fundamentalism', if you will.

It is a charge which cannot be ignored, but nor can it be answered by giving up on all issues of truth, reality and revelation. An inclusive Church only deserves to grow and thrive if it believes it is called into being by what is and what ought to be. It will seek to make this claim rationally, experientially and self-critically, not from an unassailable position of authority. But it will make its claim nonetheless.

The inclusive Church is heir to the best of the liberal Christian tradition, which it seeks to extend and deepen. At its best, liberalism witnesses to a very biblical longing for fullness of life, and to the emancipation of humanity and the earth from the unjust exercise of power. This 'social gospel' liberalism had the capacity to inspire and shape both Church and society. Valid criticisms of the shortcomings of liberalism should not blind us to its enduring achievements (one of which is the creation of places where such debates can be conducted freely and without intimidation).

Nevertheless, for too long liberal Christians have been hampered by the methodological politeness of their position, which can end in emphasizing tolerance above all else. In historical context, the appeal to tolerance has been a necessary move in ending religious wars and persecution, and, latterly, in resisting racism and encouraging respect in a diverse society. Tolerance alone, however, is not enough. It can become a cloak for the silencing of dissent and difference. It can lull us into misplaced optimism about the 'progress' of civilization, or an apathetic indifference to claims of truth and value, while destructive forces reign unchecked over our ecologies and economies.

Inclusive theology should not therefore be seen simply as liberal theology by another name. Whereas liberal theology valued reason above all else, inclusive theology is motivated principally by biblical values of justice and the transformative gospel of the kingdom. In other words, the inclusive theologian has convictions. Whether these convictions are reasonable is not the point. Nor is it relevant whether these convictions offend the prevailing secular wisdom. Our passion for an inclusive social order must be explained and accounted for, certainly, it must be debated and discussed, but it is not seeking anyone's approval.

To speak, then, of an inclusive Church is an act of *dissent* and *resistance* in a context (in both the Church as a whole and the world) where violence, prejudice and narrow claims to identity and ownership are defacing God's image in humankind and desecrating God's creation. It is an act of *affirmation* of those whose voices and experiences have been ignored and suppressed on spurious grounds. It is a celebration of the gospel of *hospitality*, which stands in judgement upon our resentments, our scapegoating and our fortress mentality.

Neo-Conservative Objections

The historic churches have been the site for many struggles over the past two hundred years. They have taken place over such things as the place of biblical criticism, the abolition of slavery, full equality and empowerment for women, acceptance of people of different sexual orientations, opposition to poverty and war, dialogue between denominations and with other religious traditions, the value placed on culture, matter, embodiment and art. What we now call the 'inclusive Church' is shaped by all these ongoing disputes and explorations. It is involved in very specific issues – the ordination of women as priests and bishops, for instance, or the promotion of blessings for same-sex couples. It can therefore be hard to locate and define, dispersed as it is throughout and beyond the major Christian denominations. Is it a movement? An idea? A dream?

To its detractors, inclusive theology is simply a capitulation to secular pressures. It is, so the charge goes, a dilution of revelation and tradition in order to appease the spirit of the age: the inclusive Church is simply a fad, turning this way and that with the meander of every cultural current. 'Inclusive theology' is, they say, a mark of the decadence of liberal Christendom which has given up on the unique Christian message and replaced it with a mish-mash of secular theories drawn from psychotherapy, sociology and other humanisms. The gospel of late Western capitalism has replaced the Good News of Jesus Christ. Instead of reading the world through the lens of Christian teaching, they say, we read Christianity through the lens of secular reason. Liberals love to talk about 'inclusion', it is said, because they no longer really want to talk about 'God' or 'revelation'. Instead, the inclusive Church tries to make Christianity conform to the standards of a world obsessed with ideas of fairness, liberty, equality, modernity and progress.

The correct response to secularization, say our neo-conservative critics, is opposition. 'Let courage rise with danger', as the hymn urges, 'and strength to strength oppose.' Being authentically Christian means that we have to set limits, define territory, defend positions and impose boundaries. Surrounded as we are by such powerful secular ideologies, the Church must show how the Christian message is different. And if one speaks up for 'the Christian difference', then exclusive claims must be made. As John Milbank argues: 'Christianity's universalist claim that incorporation into the Church is indispensable for salvation assumes that other religions and social groupings, however virtuous-seeming were finally on the path of damnation.'[1] It may offend our delicate secular feelings of 'mutual respect', but an authentic Christianity is one that is prepared to acknowledge that whole categories of humanity – the 'other religions and social groupings' – are going to hell. This, say the neo-orthodox, is the essential Christian difference: between the saved and the damned. We must draw a line between Christians and everybody else, rather in the way that the English used to distinguish between 'us' and 'foreigners'.

Because Christians are in possession of the one and only truth, Milbank argues that it is our responsibility to tell everyone else where they are going wrong:

A gigantic claim to be able to read, criticise and say what is going on in other societies, is absolutely integral to the Christian

Church, which itself claims to exhibit the exemplary form of human community. For theology to surrender this claim, to allow that other discourses – 'the social sciences' – carry out yet more fundamental readings, would therefore amount to a denial of theological truth. [2]

The neo-orthodox vision of the Church means that we, and we alone, are the universal arbiters of truth. Ideas, insights and ethics in other religions, or secular organizations, are correct only in so far as they resemble Christian teaching.

And this is where inclusive theology goes so badly wrong, say our critics: the ethic of 'inclusion' is not really rooted in Christian theology at all, but derives from 'secular' theories of natural justice or human rights. A properly Christian ethic would begin with a 'theological' concern for revelation and holiness. According to this view at least, Christianity teaches that human life is sacred because God has created us, not because we possess mysterious 'rights' or have any 'natural' entitlement to be treated with respect. We respect others not because of any intrinsic human value, but because of the value they derive from God. The appeal to 'rights' is either just a human invention, or else a form of backdoor theology that dare not speak its name.

Although this critique is fundamentally misguided, it is important that we acknowledge the germ of truth in the neo-orthodox analysis. It is easy enough for inclusive theology to look like a piecemeal reaction to external pressures to grant full rights of membership to a range of excluded groups. Instead of asserting a theological identity of its own, the inclusive Church can appear to be taking its lead from the latest secular issues. After all, where were the Christian campaigners for women's rights, or gay rights, before the twentieth century? Why was the ordination of women suddenly such an important theological issue in post-war Anglicanism? If these and other issues are so central to the Christian message – as we inclusive theologians claim – then why have they featured so little in the Church's long and complex history?

It is simply a matter of fact that inclusive theology has often presented itself in the form of short-term campaigns – the ordination of women, gay bishops, Jubilee 2000, access to church facilities – rather than enduring patterns of ecclesial life. Critics may reasonably ask whether inclusive theology will simply disappear once it has worked its way through its shopping list of organizational demands. Is there anything more substantial to 'inclusive theology' than a structural reform agenda for the Church with a few theological reflections thrown in? Where does inclusive theology go once we have an acceptable quota of lesbian archbishops and Braille hymnbooks in all our churches?

This may be frivolously put, but it is not a frivolous question. By hitching our wagons too closely to issue-driven campaigns, inclusive theology risks long-term irrelevance. Inclusive theologians must show that their concern with particular issues flows from a compelling theological vision and a foundational understanding of the inclusive identity of Christianity. We must show that the issues of inclusion are driven by theology and not vice versa.

Having said that, the development of theologies of 'this' or 'that' – feminist theology, gay theology, black theology, and so on – has been a very necessary part of uncovering Christianity's implicit theology of inclusion. And it has also been important to identify the specific categories of humanity who are excluded by any prevailing society. This process of unmasking and analysing patterns of exclusion has resulted in theologies focused upon specific groups and their needs. But there is also a need to stand back from specific inclusion issues at the same time as reaffirming their importance. In this way inclusive theology can aspire to explain how inclusion is integral to all Christian theology, not just to campaigns for the administrative reform of orders of ministry or other church policies.

Crucially, this endeavour is not limited to a single church 'party'. We believe that there are many – from open evangelicals to progressive Catholics, from thoughtful traditionalists to campaigning reformers – who share this vision and are part of this conversation. The Bible, the sacraments, the traditions and ministry of the Church are not the property of one group. Nor are they the preserve of the inward-looking who shun contact with the world out there. By immersing ourselves more deeply in these core elements of Christian faith, we believe we will be renewed in our calling to engage with God's world.

Theology Facing the World

Over forty years ago, when John Robinson wrote *Honest to God*, he did so out of a deep calling to the mission of the Church. Robinson realized that above all else religious people must be real if they are to cut any ice with an increasingly sceptical late-modern culture. 'I am not wedded to the religious language,' he argued, 'but I am deeply concerned for the reality of God.'[3] An inclusive Church must be no less honest, and no less passionate about its commitment to real theological encounter.

Unfortunately the politics of ecclesiastical truth was – and still is – such that John Robinson was accused by many of evacuating religion of theology in the vain hope that the Church could be rescued by jettisoning God. In fact Robinson – like Tillich, Bultmann and Bonhoeffer – was not trying to dispense with

God but was struggling to make the language of theology work. Like Tillich, Robinson worried that 'the words which are most used in religion are also those whose genuine meaning is almost completely lost and whose impact on the human mind is negligible'.[4] In response to this Tillich's strategy was not to abandon God but to 're-establish [the] ... original meaning and power'of theology.[5] In the same spirit, John Robinson was seeking a language which would connect the demanding heart of the gospel with the yearnings and questioning of his contemporaries.

We are unashamed in celebrating the legacy of Robinson – and the host of his forebears that stretch back to the Old Testament prophets – both in his insistence upon a theology of human reality and in his search for words and symbols and passions which might evoke the ancient gospel challenge in our day. If our task is different from his, it is because we must face new issues and questions, and draw on new resources for re-stating the Christian gospel at the beginning of the twenty-first century. The common thread is the spirit of missionary dialogue and transformative listening which must be embedded in our approach.

The writing of inclusive theology therefore proceeds very differently from neo-orthodoxy. The inclusive theologian is open to the full resources of human culture and not merely the teachings and narratives of his or her own religion. The idea that theological truth is confined to the Church is doctrinally absurd, because it limits the freedom of God to reveal truth in other ways. Rather than lock herself in a Christian citadel, the inclusive theologian breathes the fresh air of a cosmos full of opportunities for theological encounter. Moreover, the inclusive theologian is open to the theological possibilities of human culture and history. Creation is not static, after all, but unfolds in and across time.

This outward-looking stance is not a denial of Christian truth, but rather an affirmation of the inclusion, universalism, hospitality, generosity and catholicity which is dyed in the wool of Christian theology. Christianity is distinctive precisely because of its radical theology of inclusion and its ethical orientation towards the stranger and outcast. An authentic Christianity seeks to break down boundary partitions rather than to put them up. The neo-conservative impulse is always to reduce Christian living to the exercise of protocols: whether the regulation of rituals, the policing of rules or the repetition of an archetypal narrative. The tactical mistake of neo-conservatism is the belief that Christianity is best preserved by laws and fortifications: dogmas, rules, traditions.

By contrast, inclusive theology is characterized by adventure and risk, and the metaphors that come readily to mind are those of quest, exploration and pilgrimage. The relationship between faith and risk is emphasized again and again in scripture: from Abram's journey to Paul's insistence that we must live the life of the Spirit rather than a life of rules and traditions. Paul says that the Christian life is characterized by a special form of religious liberty – a liberty to pursue the truth of Jesus Christ beyond the precincts of any tradition. The risk of faith is taking the step to live without the reassurance of religious rules. This is not to say, Paul underscores, that religious doctrines and traditions are redundant. But we must not be enslaved by religious practices. Paul's inclusive instincts come through again and again as he prioritizes the spirit over the letter, extends the gospel to the gentiles and insists on the equality of slaves and women.

The inclusive theologian, like her liberal forebears, sees the relationship with secular thought as creative. This relationship does not consist of the Church handing out lectures to the world, but is a dialogue between equals in which the Church is open to what it can learn. The inclusive theologian does not recognize the allegedly stark 'difference' between secular and ecclesial reasoning, and does not assume that secular thinking automatically presents a threat to theology. We do not attempt to pull rank on the world by claiming that theology is 'the queen of the sciences', or assume that theology holds all the trump cards in the debate about God. We do not use 'secular' as a lazy pejorative. In short, the inclusive theologian does not share the current neo-conservative paranoia about all things secular.

So the relationship between the development of secular ethics and the surfacing of inclusion issues within the Church is no coincidence. Furthermore, there is not any point in denying that the churches' current concern with inclusion has come about because of the success of campaigns to have the rights of women, black people and other excluded groups recognized within secular society. The Church has, to its shame, not been at the leading edge of the development of an inclusive ethics, but has been limping slowly, and mostly reluctantly, behind leadership in the secular world. Sadly, it has taken others to remind the Church of its own true identity. The rights campaigns outside the Church have awakened the Church to its own theology of liberation and inclusion – just as Jesus, more than once, used the example of Samaritans to illustrate the true ethics of Judaism.

The reawakening of inclusive theology is one of the most exciting developments in contemporary theology, and it is only just beginning. The discussion of, say, the episcopate of Gene Robinson has stirred up the cultural memory of a primal Christian theology of inclusion. This debate has not just been about a particular North American bishop but about the theology that authorizes the existence of an inclusive Church in which gay bishops preside. Gene Robinson's consecration was not a victory in some petty struggle to get the Church to become more politically correct. This event was one sign of the Church coming into its own, the anamnesis of the Christian theology of inclusion. Like all truly significant ecclesial developments, the consecration of a gay bishop was in essence the expression of an antique theological wisdom.

This book cannot claim to be a systematic defence of inclusive theology, not least because we are suspicious of grand systems of thought which risk taking leave of reality. Rather, it attempts to be true to the spirit of dialogue, which we believe must be at the heart of all thinking about God and the world. At the same time, we hope it will demonstrate that the inclusive Church cannot simply be written off as a novelty. It is rooted in a searching reflection on the nature of human experience, shaped by response to Christian revelation and sustained by a living tradition. It is not driven by a desire to be fashionable or convenient (no more at least than any other fallible human community, whatever its supernatural claims about itself). It is formed by a developing vision and experience of what is true and good, and it calls for a costly discipleship. If we are serious about inclusion, we will have to accept that it does not come cheap.

We will attempt to articulate what has remained implicit in many of the debates about the inclusive Church. We will offer a provisional reading of human experience as it relates to revelation, and specifically to the life, death and resurrection of Jesus Christ. Our essential claim will be that inclusion is not just another theological concept to jostle alongside the others. Rather, it describes the basic dynamic of the Christian revelation.

This book is therefore organized around the central themes of Christian theology, rather than a list of current inclusion issues. In this way we hope to explore the founding theological bases for the discussion of inclusive ethics and ecclesiology. If the history of the past hundred years is any guide, then we must suppose that the specific inclusion issues of future generations will be different from our own. Indeed, there is every reason to suppose that they will be even more challenging. How will the Church deal, for example, with claims for recognition from artificial intelligences? If we think that sounds fanciful, just think for a moment whether our Victorian ancestors would have imagined the current debates about homosexuality or transgendered persons.

But this makes inclusive theology sound too much like the child of modernity. This book is also trying to show that inclusion has always been part of the grammar and instincts of Christian theology. The task of including 'the other', even the unacknowledged 'other' within ourselves, has always been fundamental to Christian living. This task involves the unsettling examination of our own insecurities, prejudices, fears and hatreds. It also involves sacrificial changes to our habits and behaviours. Because there will always be aliens – those who by dint of their strangeness, or shortage of power and numbers, are unloved and unforgiven, unheard and unrecognized, despised and rejected – there will always be an inclusive challenge facing the Church. This challenge is twofold: an internal challenge to our ecclesial attitudes and prejudices, and an external challenge to transform the world into the likeness of God's kingdom. The challenge of including the other is not new, and yet comes to us always in the form of new outcasts. One year the leper, the next the victim of AIDS – the figure of the reject is perennial and yet always takes the form of a particular person, with a name and a unique story. So, too, the theology of inclusion, which was woven into the ancient texture of Christian thought, is continually being written to include the names and voices of the newly excluded.

The Inclusive Bible

The historic tradition of inclusion has its origins, inevitably, in scripture and in the person of Jesus Christ. There is much that needs to be said about the way that the practice of an inclusive theology flows from the texts of scripture – but only a very few of these things can be covered in this short book. It is important to say, before anything else, that the Bible is the prime authority for an inclusive theology. The accusation from some quarters that inclusive theologians do not take scripture 'seriously' is quite mistaken. The inclusive Church derives its vision and authority directly from the Bible. What our critics mean is that we do not interpret the Bible to their liking, which is a different thing altogether. What people tend to mean when they say 'You don't take scripture seriously' is 'I don't agree with you'.

Taking scripture *seriously* does not mean that we have to reach an interpretation that pleases, for example, the Council of Reform, the latest self-appointed Protestant arbiter of truth, or the Congregation for the Doctrine of the Faith. We take scripture seriously by making a dedicated reading of the biblical texts and by offering a careful and reflective interpretation of their meaning. We express our 'seriousness' by the quality of our engagement with the texts, not by reaching particular conclusions.

A useful word in contemporary philosophical theology is 'incommensurability', meaning the inability to reduce a complex structure, or complex ideas, down to a single substance or simple components. As serious readers of the Bible, we should notice and respect the incommensurability of scripture. For example, the methodology of the New Testament is theological pluralism: we are offered four separate Gospels and a host of other texts, all written for different audiences. The very structure of the New Testament reveals a theological practice which values differences: differences in voice, inflection, genre and interpretation. If we are to respect scripture properly, we must take these differences seriously and understand what the richness and complexity of this assembly of texts is revealing to us.

The proper response to the incommensurability of scripture is what we could call 'hermeneutic humility', by which we mean that all interpretation of scripture is provisional and is made in the knowledge that many other, equally serious, interpretations are possible. Indeed, since the reading of scripture is always made from the point of view of readers located in different times and cultures, the ongoing interpretation of the biblical texts is necessarily open-ended. When we reach an understanding of scripture we must realize that another person may already have, or is about to have, an interpretation that does not fit with ours. This pluralism of texts and interpretations is, of course, blindingly obvious. But nevertheless the Church has still struggled to acknowledge it.

The reduction of scriptural truth to a set of doctrinal propositions is an act of vandalism on the biblical texts. Although this approach is very often held up as the mark of those who take the Bible 'seriously', it is in fact the work of those who take *dogma* seriously and are prepared to do whatever it takes to press scripture into the service of a particular church's doctrines. We only need to survey the history of the Christian denominations to see that those who claim to be taking scripture 'seriously' can reach quite different conclusions. Indeed, on the basis of these conclusions Christians have been prepared to commit some acts of terrible violence.

It is part of the genius of Christianity that it has not sought to iron out the kinks in the accounts of Jesus. We accept the absolute disagreement between John's chronology and that of the synoptics. The fact that the synoptics put the cleansing of the temple before Jesus' arrest and John puts it at the outset of Jesus' ministry has been no obstacle to faith. And this goes for numerous other differences of fact, emphasis and interpretation. We celebrate these differences because the Christian instinct has, at its best, been pluralistic. The Bible is a multi-document archive that cannot be reduced to a single theological message – although the churches have certainly tried hard enough down the ages to bring about such a reduction. All the while, scripture has remained stubbornly incommensurable – and this book, for all its passionate convictions about inclusion, will do nothing to change that.

So it is scripture itself which sets the agenda for how we read it. Not only is it pluralistic, but it shows how revelation becomes part of a living, developing tradition. The Bible is the record of an ongoing conversation, in which authors complement, correct and struggle with the insights of their predecessors. How should we worship? Should we sacrifice to God? What are the limits of our love? Which people and nations are part of God's purposes? These are just some of the fundamental questions which biblical authors answer in different ways, as they try to be true to what God is showing them in the history and experience of their day. The Bible is simply not the kind of book that turns us into passive recipients of ready-made dogma. As Jacob wrestled with God at Penuel to rediscover his relationship to the God of his forebears, so we are invited to wrestle with biblical revelation in faithfulness to its own inner dynamic.

The American Catholic theologian David Tracy has suggested a helpful way of understanding the relationship that we have with the complex reality of scripture. Tracy argues that scripture constitutes 'the Christian classic'. A 'classic' is a text which exemplifies the essence of a culture, or an artistic movement, or a particular artist's oeuvre. We may say that Shakespeare has 'classical' status in English literature, or that Pelé was a 'classic' footballer. The 'classic', as the word implies, defines the essence of an entire 'class' of cultural objects. So for Christians the scriptural texts are classics, as is the life of Jesus, and to a lesser extent the lives of the saints. The classics transcend their place in history and take on a timeless quality.

But the classic has a further quality, argues Tracy: a classic remains fascinating because it possesses an excess of meaning that will not allow itself to be reduced to any definition: 'every classic contains its own plurality and encourages a pluralism of readings'.[6] So the Bible, as our 'religious classic', expresses the tradition not by regulation but by providing the resources for a conversation about what it means to be Christian. The 'classic' shapes and influences the progress of discussion rather than offering laws and definitions.

This means that the Church is a community in discussion about its classic texts and persons. This discussion is already well underway and has 2,000 years of wisdom, and error, under its belt. But it is not over. The conversations and arguments about the essence of Christianity are still a work continually in progress. And this book is offered as a contribution to this conversation, not as a further attempt to close it down.

1

Creation

Something Given: A Starting Point for Theology

Paul speaks of Christian life as having the character of a 'new creation'. In John's Gospel, Jesus speaks of being born anew, or born from above. It is possible to read these words in a way that emphasizes the separation of Christians from the world. But this is to miss an essential point. 'New' creation can only be understood in relation to the wider question of what it means to be created in the first place. The new birth offered by the gospel is made possible by the same Spirit that is present in the very conception of the world. In other words, these powerful images are more than redundant metaphors. They speak of a deep and actual connection between Christian existence and all created reality. The newness of the life of faith does not simply abolish what went before. It makes us alive to the gifted nature of human life as such – and indeed of the whole world of which we are part.

If any aspect of theology can prevent Christianity becoming parochial, or the property of an elect few, it is the doctrine of creation. Here, we can see clearly how Christian theology has insisted upon values and principles of inclusion. Inclusion, not as an abstract law or pious sentiment, but as rooted in the character of what *is*. The doctrine of creation is not only where Christian theology begins, but where inclusive theology begins, because the fact of our created existence is something we share with every other human being – indeed with all life, all matter. It is because we are created that we are morally and spiritually connected, opened to an otherness beyond anything we have initiated or have under our control. Inclusion, therefore, is not about gathering everything into a uniform system. It is a deep sharing in networks of relationship that take us beyond our narrow, distorted, me-and-my-tribe ideas of reality. Inclusion in this liberating relationship of creation is *grace*.

Of course, our sense of what 'is' will always be mediated and interpreted through language, culture, politics. It's never simply 'there', because our humanity finds its expression in such diverse, partial and changing ways. It may be that we do not think of ourselves, explicitly, as 'created'. But we will have some other way of speaking about the fact that we exist. We may use the language of 'gift' and simply say that our existence has been 'given' to us in some mysterious way. We sometimes say, without any religious intention, that we are 'put here on earth'. Or we may use the language of discovery and speak of 'finding' that we are alive in the cosmos. Heidegger said rather dramatically that we are 'thrown into the world'. Darwin bequeathed us another metaphor, having us think that we have 'evolved' into the world.

These metaphors struggle to reflect the fact that existing is something that *happens to us*. We do not choose to exist or will ourselves into being. Existence feels like something 'given' or 'found' or 'thrown'. In some sense, our existence is something we 'receive'. We may not credit a creator with responsibility for our existence, but we cannot credit ourselves with it either. So we are left looking for words that can communicate the feeling of 'otherness' about our lives. Nothing could be more familiar to us than our own bodies, thoughts and feelings, but there is also a strange quality to them. Where did we get ourselves from?

Looking around at the world we ask: where did all this stuff come from?

These questions are not in themselves theological, although their theological possibilities are obvious. These are questions of basic curiosity. We ask them because the fact of existence is astonishing. So when we speak about being 'created' we are, to start with, simply finding words to express the phenomenon of being alive in the world. The language of creation, properly used, is not so much a statement about God (although God is implicated in it) as a way of speaking about this strange 'given' quality of the existing world of which we are part. To say we are 'created' communicates something of our gratitude, astonishment or confusion about the fact that we exist at all.

It is from the experience of being a 'created' person that we begin to think theologically. There is no other place to start because our existence is the precondition of every other starting point. If we try to begin theology with God, Jesus, the Bible or anything else we will already have presupposed our original questioning existence. If there is no human being to ask the theological questions, then theology cannot get started. Theology starts with questioning, and questioning requires the existence of a person to ask the questions.

This is not, as might appear, a version of humanism. Saying that theology depends upon human existence is not the same thing as saying that God depends upon human existence. Having said that, the human starting point for theology clearly does not rule out humanistic conclusions. By starting theology with creation – that's to say, by starting it with the simple truths of our human existence – we are providing theology with its first solid ground and ensuring that theology is not merely speculative. In conventional religious terms, our existence is a point of revelation: it is the first thing that God gives us to think about.

The mysterious quality of feeling 'created' is universal. This is the common denominator that brings together not only every human person, but every existent thing. This is our fundamental link with other people, *all* other people *whoever* they are. It is from this platform that we construct our ideas of responsibility, ideal community, ethics, rights, and even our idea of God.

This idea of a universal, created humanity is now an everyday concept. We speak of the 'brotherhood of man', or the human race. The Universal Declaration of Human Rights talks about 'the human family'. Rousseau spoke of the fundamental equality of humanity and Marx spoke of 'species-being'. Although this idea has been taken up with particular enthusiasm in the modern period, the idea of a universal humanity is not a secular invention – as the neo-conservatives would have us believe – but a basic Christian concept. Christians have always believed in the fundamental equality of human beings under God – even if the Church in practice has not often lived up to this belief.

The Judeo-Christian creation myth imagines that the diverse peoples of the earth are descended from original human parents. Adam and Eve stand for all humanity – from them are descended every Christian, Jew and Muslim, every lesbian and gay man, every atheist. This is inclusive humanity. This common humanity is our fundamental bond with people of every kind.

This is a crucial point. The theology we are proposing does not fall from the sky as a set of timeless, abstract truths. Our sense of what is real, our sense of God, is bound up with our active, living questions, and with our ethical bonds with other people and with all life. It is the Other who calls us into being. This rules out the narrow dogmatism which always tries to speak for and dominate the Other. And it sets the tone for our project, which must always, from before the beginning, be a theology with and for the Other. A theology in which doctrine is never divided from living, questioning wonder, nor from an ethical commitment to the full human dignity of each person. Nothing less than this is what it means to start with creation.

Creation's Original Goodness

In a sense, of course, there is nothing new at all about this. The best Christian theology has always been in dialogue with the world. It has rejected the tidy dualism which violently dissects the rich, diverse wholeness of what is. This is why Christians have maintained that the distinctive theological feature of creation in Genesis is that it is 'good'. St Augustine makes this point very powerfully at the end of his *Confessions*. 'It is from the abundance of your goodness that your creation exists . . . all things [have] been made very good by you, the one supreme Good.'[1] Augustine says that every individual part of creation is 'good' and that the totality of creation is 'very good'. It is the uniform 'goodness' of creation that reflects the ultimate goodness of God. According to the Creation myth, nothing at all in creation is out of place or inappropriate.

Furthermore, the idea of a good creation is utterly inclusive: 'all things were made through him and without him was not anything made that was made' (John 1:3). If there is only one God, then it follows that his creation must be the only creation. God's creation includes everything that is. Anything apart from God's good creation simply can't exist.

The doctrine of the goodness of nature was one of the fiercely contested issues of the patristic period. The Gnostics offered the alternative view that creation is a mixture of good and evil parts.

22

Good and evil are locked into a cosmic battle for control of the universe. In some versions of Gnosticism there are good and evil gods fighting for world-domination. The Gnostic heresy rests upon a violent metaphysical distinction between light and darkness. Whereas Augustine had argued that darkness was simply the absence of light, the Gnostics imagined darkness to be a reality in its own right.

This theory has an intuitive appeal – after all, when we look at the world we appear to see good and evil events, happiness and suffering, good and bad people. The Gnostic view appears to fit much better with our experience. Theologians like Augustine and Irenaeus had to work hard to argue for the counter-intuitive view that, despite appearances, creation really is all good. This was a difficult case to make, with any person able to cite numerous examples of human misery, cruelty and hatred. What about cancer, earthquakes, infanticide?

The reason that Augustine fought so vociferously on this issue is that he was passionately committed to an inclusive view of creation and resisted the 'heretical' view that God would permit the creation of anything evil. If God is good, then what he has created must also be good. Everything that God makes is included equally in the goodness of creation. How could it be otherwise? Any other conclusion would be illogical, even blasphemous.

We don't need to agree with Augustine in order to appreciate the radically inclusive nature of his view of creation. The inclusive view of creation was not a marginal issue for Augustine, but a seminal theological insight that plays a crucial role in both his own spiritual autobiography and subsequent Christian theology. So we need to remember that the principle of inclusion is not a modern invention but was cast in the furnace of debate about what constituted orthodoxy. The inclusive doctrine of creation is basic Christian teaching. Don't let the neo-conservatives tell you otherwise.

Despite this, Gnostic dualism has retained its appeal through the ages and has reared its head again and again in the course of church history. This normally takes the form of some kind of demonization. Witches, heretics, perverts, wrong-doers, Jews and other infidels are no longer seen as part of God's good creation, but as enemies to be resisted, sometimes even brutally destroyed. Down the ages numerous church people have fallen under the spell of the Gnostic heresy, seeing life as a battle against the agents of evil. The task of the Gnostic Christian is to be a protector against the threats of wrong-doers, unorthodox theologians, corrupt worshippers, infidel peoples, the 'axis of evil' and a thousand other manifestations of the evil one. The gospel of love is quickly turned into a gospel of exclusion, fear and very often violence.

Today we are suffering from the resurgence of a new Gnosticism in the churches. It feeds on the insecurity bred by the fast-changing modern age. It offers a steady rock in the storm of swirling fashions, advancing science and cultural clashes. This new Gnosticism tries to erect a security fence between 'the Church' and 'the World', with Church people exclusively in possession of truth and virtue. Slowly but surely this theology fashions a God who is disconnected from the world he has created, and who communicates divine decrees only through a mysteriously sanctioned chain of ecclesiastical authority. To the Gnostic church, the world appears disenchanted, nihilistic and godless. Its followers shiver at the evils of 'secularism' and cling ever more tightly to their fragile idols.

In effect, the new Gnosticism – whether Protestant Biblicism, or certain ultra-Catholic or Orthodox idealizations of papal infallibility or unchanging tradition – creates the God it wants.

The function of this God is to answer our very human need for security by providing a safe ecclesial enclave in the modern empire of secularism. This God hides his followers from the truth of life's painful fragility and ambiguity. Ironically, the most stringent world-denying conservatism flips over into the most self-serving idolatry. God the creator is banished from his creation and exiled to the encampment of the faithful. Jesus, the incarnate God who became part of the flesh of creation, is ushered into a safe tabernacle. God's Spirit becomes a private genie serving his ecclesiastical masters.

But – and this is a big 'but' – if we reject Gnostic dualism we need to find some other way of accounting for the suffering and cruelty of the world. Belief in the goodness of creation is emphatically not the delusion that everything that happens in this world is good. As we have seen, doctrine is worked out in a spirit of open questioning, and in ethical solidarity with all humankind and with all that lives. It does not try to force reality to fit its theories and speculations. This means that we have to take seriously the reality of evil and suffering, what in Christian tradition has been considered under the heading 'the fall'.

Falling Together: Christians and Evil

The fall is probably the most widely misunderstood and wilfully distorted of all Christian doctrines. Properly understood, the idea of the fall begins with a recognition that human beings appear to be incapable of living virtuous lives. History shows us that the best efforts of the best people are incapable of producing a perfect moral world. Even in our individual lives we may wonder why we cannot bring about improvements that we strongly desire. It feels as though there is some basic flaw in human nature that keeps blocking our efforts at virtue and success.

The Genesis story of Adam and Eve offers a mythological explanation. In eating the forbidden fruit, Adam and Eve take upon themselves a moral responsibility that they are quite unable to live up to. The knowledge of good and evil brings with it the god-like responsibility for exercising ethical choices. But the making of perfect ethical choices requires a knowledge of all things, of the causes and effects of every action (including those in the future), of the hidden thoughts and feelings of others, and the ability to act unselfishly. If there is such a thing as a perfect ethics then it could only be achieved by a god.

We live in an ambiguous and conflicted moral universe where ethics must be worked out as best we can. The moral decisions we take are difficult and rarely result in ideal outcomes. This is our world, the world of the fall. And we are all in it together. The doctrine of the fall is as emphatically inclusive as the doctrine of a good creation: every person lives in the fallen world. 'The fallen' are not a sub-set of humanity who we can pity, patronize or even abuse. The category of the fallen takes in the whole human race. And because we are all caught in fallenness, there is no moral high ground from which we can judge others. The doctrine of the fall denies the legitimacy of 'holier-than-thou' religion. This is not supposed to be a depressing or negative idea. It is, rather, a form of realism: the acceptance of moral facts. Look around, or pick up a history book, and we'll see it's true.

In fact the Christian idea of the fall is also realistically *hopeful*, because it imagines that our present moral incapacity is 'a fall' from an earlier state of created grace. In some imagined human pre-history – the mythical Garden of Eden – everything was perfect. This need not be taken literally in any sense for us to recognize its force. The fall marks a decisive moment in human development, a moment of ethical self-consciousness: the awareness of the imperfection of the world on the one hand, and the glimpses of an ideal world-order on the other.

Because we have a sense of being 'created' we are driven to ask questions. There is something about the gifting of life to us which makes us ask moral questions, questions of love, justice, purpose and fulfilment which go beyond the brute facts of mere existence. We sense a range of human possibilities and potentialities that lie unrealized. We have an intuition that human life is currently less than it should be.

This might be called a capacity for transcendence: the ability to go beyond what is given, instinctive, inarticulate. Among modern theologians, perhaps Karl Rahner has done most to advance a view of the human person as a 'transcendent being': all of our knowing and acting takes place within the horizon of infinite being. For Rahner, this does not mean that we are cut off from the rest of creation. We experience the transcendence of being in and through the material world and our historical life.

This transcendence is, therefore, a deeply ambiguous trait. It does allow us to develop a free moral and spiritual openness to new dimensions of otherness – whether of the world, people or God. However, it also presents us with opportunities for deceit, extravagant cruelty, and domination beyond anything inherent in natural evolution. When we are no longer driven by necessity and instinct, the vertigo-inducing void of freedom beckons us. Kierkegaard and other philosophers have identified this as the dizzying experience of anxiety or angst, which is not a fear about this or that particular situation, but the dread which shadows our basic human capacity for moral choice. Every human life stages this drama, poses this question, walks suspended between time and eternity.

The story of the fall identifies the eating of the fruit of knowledge with the moment when human beings become self-aware. That moment is associated with shame, and with a compensating lust for exclusive god-like power (particularly striking in the subsequent stories of Cain's murder of Abel and the building of the Tower of Babel). At the same time, it is also a moment of hope – that the dream of the garden will be realized.

No doubt there is something here of nostalgia for a mythical golden age of innocence, maybe of a return to the womb from which nature and culture have torn us. But there is more to this than mere wish-fulfilment. At the heart of our anxiety and our delusions, there is a sense that things can be different. Relationships – with one another, with animal life, with nature – *can* be non-violent and non-possessive. The birth of self-consciousness offers hope, for a new immediacy, a new creation. This is a hope for a life fuller and richer because it has learnt to face anxiety, mortality and vulnerability, without surrendering what Paul Tillich once called the 'courage to be'. To live with an honest recognition of human corruption, without ever losing hold of this hope and courage; to live out of the generosity of creation's gift, rather than the self-defensiveness of fear and domination: this is the vision to which a Christian doctrine of creation and fall calls us.

So in sum, the Christian doctrine of creation runs like this: we share a common humanity with every other person. And each and every one of us is a 'good' creation. This inclusive human solidarity is prior to all our cultural differences and lifestyle choices. But we are not only united as creatures, we are united in the struggle to make moral sense of our ambiguous human world. The doctrine of the fall asserts that no person has a monopoly on the truth or ethics. We are all included in the debate about the nature of the truth and of right conduct. And this suggests that creation is not over and done with, but is an ongoing process of dialogue. The word which calls light forth in the Genesis myth does not drop stillborn in an empty void, but creates beings and voices which resonate with and respond to the gift of life. Creation replaces immobile and monotonous deadness with the unpredictable song of living being.

This sense of the unpredictability and the risk of creation might help us in looking beyond the evident reality of human moral evil, to what can seem even more troubling and mysterious. What Christian theologians call 'natural evil' encompasses all those elements of disease and disaster, and the preying of life upon life, through which so much suffering is caused. Human evil and injustice can often trigger or compound the effects of such disaster, as when the poorest suffer most in earthquakes or the lack of treatment for disease. The most humanly possible perfect ordering of society would still be subject to natural calamity and bodily decay. What place does this have in all our talk about human freedom, transcendence and openness?

The simple truth is that there is no adequate intellectual 'explanation' of natural evil. Pat answers about the will of God or demonic influence simply reveal how insensitive and unreal such explanations can be. However, it is helpful when considering natural evil to distinguish between the terms 'evil' and 'tragedy'. When we use the word 'evil' we normally mean that suffering has been intended – either deliberately or by neglect. With evil there is always culpability. But when we speak of 'tragedy' we normally mean a form of suffering which has not been wished for. Thus murder is 'evil', but manslaughter is 'tragic'. If you die at the hands of a torturer, that's evil. If you die in surgery at the hands of a doctor, that's tragic. We reserve the word 'evil' for deliberate and cruel acts, and use the word 'tragedy' to describe accidental or unintended suffering.

The question, then, is whether we describe natural disasters and illnesses as 'evil' or 'tragic'. If we choose to use the word 'evil' to describe cancer we are presented with the problem of saying who is responsible for intending the suffering. Is it God? Does God require certain people to suffer a premature and painful death? If so, how does God select his victims from the multitude of potential candidates? These questions show that regarding natural suffering as 'evil' can only lead to a speculative chaos in which unanswerable questions pile upon unanswerable questions. Since it is impossible to say how, let alone why, God would want to intend suffering, it is better, perhaps, to view so-called natural evil as 'tragedy': a form of suffering without any obvious culpability. This then permits us to ask a different question: why does the created order contain so many tragic features?

One tentative answer comes from the inherent risk in the act of creation. This risk is a necessary counterweight to freedom. If we agree that a good creation is one that is free, then we need to accept the tragic accidental effects of this freedom. Human beings could only come into existence in a world which was not simply a puppet of divine forces, but which was allowed to evolve through uncountable chance factors and local adaptations. The corollary of receiving life as a morally and spiritually meaningful gift is a recognition of its vulnerability, and of the tragic shadow that accompanies our hopes.

Facing this question – though we know answers turn to ash in our mouth – is vital for an inclusive theology. We have seen how Gnostic dualism, in old and new forms, cuts us off from the gift of creation, and maroons us on a fantasy island of security. Extreme readings of the doctrine of the fall play the same game. Human beings are seen as totally depraved, and only an elect few are snatched to safety by arbitrary divine decree. In the same way, a failure to accept the vulnerability and tragedy that are part of human life is an attempt to escape the real world. It is a delusion that we (again, usually a privileged inner group) can explain anything and everything that happens as the result of human or supernatural decisions. It reduces creation to an empty shell, with no substance of its own. History becomes a charade and God is made a puppet-master, whose plans always seem to favour one group at the expense of others.

Human insecurity forces the doctrines of creation and fall into a narrow interpretative straitjacket. An inclusive theology seeks to be faithful to those doctrines as rich, living realities of human experience. It has no truck with the puppet-master God, created in the image of our own wishes. Instead, it seeks the truly creative God, God's own risk of making and relating to something new. This mysterious, compelling and challenging God is met in and through the stuff of life and history. And we see no reason to accept that any person or group has an inbuilt advantage in relating to this God. It is in our common humanity, our worldly and transcendent humanity, that belief in creation has its source, and upon which it grows.

Transforming Inclusion: Learning a New Creation

At this point in the argument, we need to pause and recognize an objection from another source. What if our fallenness manifests itself in such a fundamentally *broken* humanity as to make all talk of universal values and commonality suspect at best – and a dangerous delusion at worst? Bland optimism about human nature and progress died in the mud of Flanders and was cremated in the ovens of Auschwitz. It has also been taken to task for justifying the inequalities of the status quo. The flourishing of movements of liberation in the last century has found it necessary to challenge some of the preconceptions of grand univer-sal stories. We have learnt to ask where these stories and values come from and whose interests they serve. It's all very well talk-ing about everyone being part of a debate and a conversation, as if all that needed to happen was to set another place at the table. The reality is that our anxiety-driven systems of exclu-sion, domination and control can make it impossible for many to take that place, or even to be recognized as fully human.

Our inclusive reading of the doctrines of creation and fall can therefore be criticized by those who have found themselves not only on the margins of secular and church power and privilege, but on the receiving end of systems of exclusion, prejudice and violence. Over the last few decades, the underground resistance of oppressed communities – women, blacks, landless peasants, the urban poor, lesbians, gay men, bisexuals, the transgendered and more – have found more explicit, radical voices.

These voices have, in different ways, exposed the structures of domination lurking in the heart of the Western dream. They have not been content to call for individual reforms or attack disconnected abuses. Their targets have been the presupposi-tions behind whole systems of symbolic and actual power: the patriarchy which associates men with spirit, intellect and power, and which calls for women's bodies and minds to be controlled and domesticated; the Eurocentrism and white supremacism which has justified colonialism and slavery and which continues to feed racist attitudes and institutions; the heterosexism, which dismisses as perverse and unclean all people and behaviours which do not fit what it considers 'normal'; the condescension of the able-bodied, who continue to dehumanize the disabled, and describe evil in terms of 'blindness' and 'deafness'.

In short, these voices have not just demanded a seat at the table. They have called for the tables themselves to be overthrown, for unjust structures to be challenged and transformed root and branch. In this context, the idea of 'inclusion' can easily appear to be another well-meaning ruse, by which the privileged appear to be generous, without ever fundamentally calling their own status and prestige into question. Inclusion can become the patronizing gesture of those who consider themselves to be insiders, inviting in those poor unfortunates who languish at their gates. But this type of 'hospitality' never upsets the real balance of power, the sense that the outsiders must be for ever grateful that they were 'let in'. It assumes that there is nothing wrong with any institution which a little more openness cannot cure. It complacently says 'Come and join us – as long you become *like* us.'

So women must slot into a hierarchy created by male power; gays must ape straight relationships; bisexuals and the transgendered must define themselves according to the fixed opposites of hetero- and homosexuality; the poor must become respectable and blacks must be washed whiter than white. And all the time, the old systems sink new roots into the freshly turned earth.

We are clear that this naive, centralized inclusion from above or from a mythical centre must be rejected. Jesus offended people when he said that the first would be last and that tax collectors and prostitutes would go before the righteous and respectable into the kingdom of God, but he was stating a simple truth. Those who think they already own the kingdom will inevitably be the last to be fully converted. That conversion happens when they learn from the experiences of those who were considered marginal, but who are now discovering themselves to be at the centre of God's empowering, liberating purpose.

Real inclusiveness, real hospitality, must radically transform our structures. It is not that a privileged 'we' have something, which we're trying to work out how best to share. It's rather that, in the polyphony of experiences and struggles for fullness of life, a new creation is coming to birth in and through and between us: the Spirit of God is weaving many languages into a new kind of community. There are many who are learning to speak in their own name – to say 'I' and 'we' as if for the first time. Those of us who belong to traditionally privileged groups have to learn to hear this strange speech, and through it to learn again what it means for our sense of who we are and where we belong. Far from being an exercise in liberal guilt, this is the road to healing truth.

Given all the temptations of ideological distortion and power games that surround claims to universal truth, it is therefore tempting to abandon any sense of a common created humanity. But this would be a fatal mistake. To surrender to fragmentation and relativism only plays into the hands of those whose interests are served by the idea that truth is simply a matter of competition and the will to power, of whose story comes out on top in the end. However inadequate and fumbling our attempts may be to talk about human rights and the sacred worth of human life, without this conviction we have no basis for resisting the powers of death and oppression in our world.

Instead, we have to ask: how and from whom do we experience creation anew as the gift that shatters the myth that there ever could be insiders and outsiders in God's life-giving purposes? To know that we are created – not just intellectually, but in our heart, in our gut – is to be changed. Recalling the themes of the New Testament to which we referred at the start of this chapter, there is no contradiction between learning who we have always been (being called by our true name) and being radically transformed (becoming a *new* creation). They are two ways of looking at the same experience, an experience embedded in the nature of what it means to be human. So we find that, in talking about creation, we have already been talking about two other hotly disputed areas of Christian teaching: revelation and salvation.

2

Revelation

The Mystery of Revelation

If we understand revelation to be the communication of privileged supernatural information, we will always end up with the elitist scenario we described previously. There will always be an in-group to whom the true facts about our human situation have been delivered, and they will always be pleading with, patronizing, judging or pushing away the world 'out there'. And there will never be a satisfactory way of answering the charge that such a God of revelation is arbitrary. He seems to choose some people rather than others to hear his words, leaving most of humanity wallowing in ignorance and sin. We are left with absurd dilemmas, forced to argue for the sake of decency that God will give those who never heard the gospel one last chance to accept Christ after they die. What a pointless charade this makes of human life on this earth. What a fickle monster it makes of God.

Equally as seriously, such a doctrine of revelation has far-reaching effects on what we mean by salvation, by that coming to fullness of life which is the goal of faith. It reduces the most profound discoveries to the accumulation of 'facts', and turns faith into a mere collection of beliefs. This is a travesty of our deepest relationships and encounters with others. I do not love my friends because I know a lot of facts about them. I love them because of a mutual commitment, recognition and vulnerability. And in the safety and nakedness of intimate friendship, in the sweat and accomplishment of shared work, in the hidden depths and shimmering surfaces of art and nature, I rediscover the world in its strange beauty. I rediscover who I am – or better, who *we are* – seen through the eyes of another.

For much of the witness of the Bible and the tradition of the Church affirms that revelation is more like an encounter than it is the learning of previously hidden information. Moreover, it is an encounter through which we find ourselves (alongside every other human being) in relation to the deepest truth and source of our being, a relation to One whose essence we never entirely grasp. There is a mystery at the heart of revelation. In the story of Jesus meeting the disciples on the road to Emmaus after the resurrection (Luke 24), he vanishes from their sight even as they recognize him for who he really is. The risen Christ can't be caged.

One of the most persistent motifs in Christian theology is that of the 'negative' way, in which we arrive at an encounter with what is most real only by denying and stripping away the partial and inadequate ideologies with which we usually attempt to capture it. Dogma should therefore never set itself up as the one and only truth, for that would be to supplant God. Language slips away from us. It is life that opens us, in ways words cannot enclose, to the mystery of being-in-relationship.

The Letter to the Ephesians says of God:

> With all wisdom and insight he has made known to us the mystery of his will, according to his good pleasure that he set forth in Christ, as a plan for the fullness of time, to gather up all things in him, things in heaven and things on earth.
>
> (Ephesians 1:8–10)

What is made known to us in Christ thus remains a mystery even as it is shared, because there is no way that our finite capacities can truly think or imagine what is being made known: that all things – *all* things – are truly what they are because they are in relationship with the creative love of God embodied in Christ, the one who 'fills all in all' (Ephesians 1:23). Small wonder that the term 'mystery' came to be attached first to the confessions of faith and creeds taught to those about to join the Church, and, secondly, to the sacramental acts of worship which forged the communion between the believers, God and the world. The creeds were not recitals of lists of supernatural facts, the sacraments were not mere 'services'. They were the dramatically enacted stories and symbols through which believers came to share in 'mystery', the calling of all things into that web of life-giving relationships which is the new covenant, the New Testament, or the new creation.

That the Church did not always live up to this vision, that it turned creeds into ideology, and sacraments into priestcraft and magic should not make us forget that the Christian doctrine of revelation – as a guide to what it means to be part of this new creation – is astonishingly inclusive, and demands recovery. The rise of scientific ways of thinking has challenged many superstitions and enlarged our sense of the reality of the world. However, it has also bequeathed certain popular prejudices: that the only truths are those that can be 'proved' by scientific techniques and stated in clear factual propositions; and that much religion is therefore a private matter of the heart. As a consequence, Christians have often tried to ape this sort of truth, turning the Bible or the Pope into a source of infallible truths which must be accepted without question. But this is distortion of the wider Christian tradition, not to mention our daily experience that it is the truth embodied in relationships that matters most, even while it escapes narrowly rationalistic definition.

To experience revelation is not to be transported out of the world, but to rediscover what it means to be created, and therefore bound in relations of solidarity with the earth and those with whom one shares it. It is not a timeless and abstract truth, but takes form in history. 'The Word became flesh' is the most startling originality that Christianity has to offer. It affirms that the Word is not defined in a scripture or church dogma, but expressed in the humanity of Christ. It also affirms that this process of the embodiment of God's word is not exhausted by the historical life of Jesus. It continues in those who are joined to him and who therefore become his body. And time and time again, the vision of the Hebrew Scriptures, of Jesus and the New Testament writers, is that this reality cannot be confined to those who call themselves 'God's people' or the 'Church'. It is found in Ruth and Rahab, Melchizedek and Jethro; it comes from Ethiopia, Persia and the wisdom of Sheba; it calls tax collectors and prostitutes its children, and is poured out on the gentiles.

Revelation is a gift. Not one that drops down from heaven, but one that beckons to us through the faces, voices and bodies of the 'other', the outsider, the one who subverts our self-contained systems of power and piety. The New Testament, seeking to register the impact of Christ on the world, confirms this. It invokes a vision of a community which abolishes hierarchy, a body made of many gifts, a numberless redeemed multitude of every race and language, the whole of creation caught up in transformation.

That dramatic movement from the Word made flesh to the community of faith, and out to the whole of creation, is well summarized in the Letter to the Colossians:

He [Christ] is the head of the body, the church; he is the begin-

39

ning, the firstborn from the dead, so that he might come to have first place in everything. For in him all the fullness of God was pleased to dwell, and through him God was pleased to reconcile to himself all things, whether on earth or in heaven, by making peace through the blood of his cross.

(Colossians 1:18–20)

The specific becoming-flesh of God in Christ is anything but the start of a new religion for the elect only. This inclusive revelation is put most succinctly by Paul, who states that 'as in Adam all die, so all will be made alive in Christ' (1 Corinthians 15:22). There it is again: *all.*

Revelation and Communication

That sense of being part of the 'all' has to be worked out in very concrete ways. As we have recognized, grand visions of universal salvation are empty if they are cloaks for ongoing exclusion and prejudice. The 'all' has to be woven out of very particular struggles for human dignity and flourishing and connection with creation. Revelation happens when we realize we no longer need to define ourselves *against* others, that we need no longer demand sacrifices and victims to secure our sense of identity. It is the clearing and living of a different way of being in the world, one which is faithful to the reality of our common creation. Christian faith, which for many is associated with maintaining institutions and upholding correct doctrines, was originally known as 'the Way' (Acts 24:22). It is something to be lived as we walk in company with others.

Earlier we referred to the story of the risen Christ disappearing from his disciples' table at the point when they recognize him. This is not only a testimony to the mystery that continually attends revelation. It is also a witness to its openness. Christ cannot be confined to one meeting point. He has other roads to walk, other tables at which to show himself as guest and host. These challenging encounters are not just a means to an end, but part of the very essence of what he is showing to us. The Emmaus Road story is a parable of what happens every time we set out on that difficult pilgrimage into living truth.

This understanding of revelation is therefore anything but a tepid, lazy unwillingness to think through difficult claims about truth and value. We are not making the inane suggestion that any and every human belief is 'revealed' or 'true'. In discussing the fall, we have underlined the need to be honest and serious about the reality of human evil and limitation. However, we are claiming that the Christian revelation is an invitation to take part in a living *way* of truth, a critical solidarity of discovery. It is not an ahistorical, rootless 'answer' to all of life's questions.

This is what gives inclusive theology substance. For we are not talking about the simple fact of believing that all will be saved, or that all are created in God's image. At issue here is the whole way we understand and practise theology.

To be more specific: revelation is not simply inclusive in its contents or results, but also in its process, the *way* it happens and affects us. The 'what' cannot be divorced from the 'how'. We can appreciate this by drawing an analogy with human communication. The same set of words or symbols or actions can have very different meaning, depending on how they are said, and in which context. The factors influencing how a communication is received and interpreted are legion: tone of voice; the power relationships between the people involved; body language; the institutional setting; cultural differences; the history of the conversation up to that point – the elements could be multiplied. The process and context of communication cannot be neatly separated from what it 'means'.

If revelation is about communication of the nature, will and presence of God, then it must be at least as rich and complex as our ordinary communications. Those daily acts of speech and gesture do much more than simply transmit information. Each one contains the seeds of whole dramas of contested history and value-making, huge assumptions about what makes sense and what doesn't. They create and sustain bonds of identity, while simultaneously opening us to what is other and new. They involve the whole person, body, mind and what we have learnt to call 'spirit' – the transcendent nature of our humanity which accompanies everything we do and say, but which can never be reduced to or translated into something obvious, direct or mundane.

Language and our other modes of communication are moral and spiritual in the very texture of their being. As such, they can mould communities into intensely felt collectives, but they can also offer the most profound innovation and challenge to the status quo. Communication thus reveals and conceals at the same time. As much as it makes people and their worlds intelligible to one another, it can't be used to construct an all-encompassing total system of life, which would put everything and everyone in their proper place. We have no God's eye view of the whole. Every language has a history. Every language is constantly evolving, developing new idioms. And every language is a mongrel creation, made up of many voices, codes and struggles, and always in dialogue and tension with other languages.

If this is true of our everyday communication, we need to consider what this suggests to us about revelation from God.

First, it suggests that there is no one timeless language or rulebook of revelation, of what it is, what it means and how it appears. The bare fact of diversity and conflict in every religious tradition that claims a revealed basis should confirm this to us. But there is a more fundamental point to be made: we simply have no idea of what such a context-free and absolute communication could be like. There is no way we could recognize it for what it is, for we are historical beings. Everything we are and do is mediated through the ebb and flow of existence in time and the shifting kaleidoscopic hues of language and symbol.

Secondly, and more positively, any revelation must be as holistic and multidimensional as our ordinary intercourse. The Christian faith has undergone many shifts of interpretation, with now one facet, now another being emphasized. But it can never be wholly reduced to, say, a literal reading of the Bible, or to the officially expounded 'tradition' of the Church, any more than it can be deduced from free-standing abstract rational principles. There has always to some extent been a rich dialogue at the heart of Christian communication. Word and sacrament, memory and hope, the respect due to the past and the living voice of the Spirit. Revelation is inclusive in this sense, too. It resists becoming a one-dimensional ideology, which an in-group can claim for its own and use at will. In the most authoritarian church, be it Protestant, Catholic or Orthodox, the way the believer receives and responds to preaching and liturgy can never wholly be controlled. Isn't this what we might expect from a faith at whose heart the Word of God becomes historical, human flesh, and whose community is guided by a Spirit which no one can pin down or contain?

Thirdly, therefore, revelation is not simply the end of all mystery, the answering of all questions. Faith is not a species of certainty, or even of knowledge in the narrow sense of that word. Far from this being a defect of faith, it is the secret of its freedom. Faith is found in relationship. It is trust and confi-

uence, yes – but to confuse it with certainty about the 'facts' is
to fall back into the old craving for security from which faith
should set us free. To find myself in deep relationship with another person is also to respect their freedom and 'mystery'. To
pursue the most passionate forms of political and social com-
mitments will turn into another power-trip unless we always
resist the temptation to bully, control and dominate others by
the force of our own programme. The problem with religious
fundamentalism therefore is that it is not respectful *enough* of
revelation. It wants something different from what God gives.
It demands that God deliver an impossible and oppressive certainty. Fundamentalism is God's bully, trying to force God into
a mould we create. It is a theological stalker, refusing to let God
be God. If we are to refuse this kind of compulsive obsession,
we need to relearn what it means *to have faith in faith*, and not
to turn it into something lesser, something made to serve our
own ends.

In sum, then, revelation is a living encounter, in which we are
set free for truthful, generous existence. It is liberating, and open
to the future. Its rootedness in the past is dynamic. It does not
trap us in the pessimistic and nostalgic prejudice that all that is
true, good and beautiful has already been said, done and lived.
We are not fated to be mere echoes and footnotes to a static tradition. Our grateful response to what wisdom and saving truth is
given in tradition must also be a grateful responsibility: to listen
to the present world's questions and confusions, to discern the
new dialects in which revelation is being expressed, to explore
the unexpected horizons of truth and error, good and evil that
are constantly opening up.

We claim that this outline of revelation is true. By this, we
don't mean it possesses some sort of pseudo-mathematical certainty, or that it translates into a systematic and absolute grasp

of reality. As far as what it means to live and exist in relationship goes, that kind of truth is a fantasy of control.

No, we mean that our view of revelation is true to the nature of the God encountered in Israel, Christ and Church; it answers to basic human dimensions of communication; it is reasonable, without being rationalistic. In other words, it is the kind of truth that matters: dynamic, compelling, but also tentative, knowing when to be silent as well as when to speak.

If Christians are not to retreat into a private sect-like mentality, they must stand on this ground: to seek and welcome the truth from wherever it comes. Otherwise, we will simply end doing what some Christian fundamentalists have done in the USA: building theme park museums to absurd doctrines like creationism, and scandalously, faithlessly, rejecting God's evolving gift of wisdom.

Revealed in the Flesh

Looking back over the ground we have covered so far, the hybrid nature of our method will be obvious. We do not draw absolutely clear lines of demarcation between creation and revelation, between our experience of the mysteries of human communication and our sharing in the life of God. This is in no way to suggest that 'God' can be reduced to a human creation or an aspect of the human psyche or a projection of social imagination. It is precisely because we believe in the genuine otherness of God that we refuse the blind alley presented by so much recent theology, which mistakes the purity of its method for the transcendence of God. Start with the uncontaminated Word of God, or the idealized Church, or the unique master Story of Christian faith, and everything falls into place – or so we are told.

The problem with these approaches is that they do not seem to have the courage to bear the actual nature of Christian revelation. Because what makes it *Christian* is also what renders all these absolutes suspect. This is a crucial point, which deserves clarification.

For some, Christianity needs to be sharply distinguished from 'natural' human insights and from alternative religious views. The uniqueness of God's revelation, culminating in the highly specific incarnation of God in one human individual, has to be preserved at all costs. Otherwise, it is argued, Christianity becomes subservient to the shifting, self-interested and corrupt flux of human cultures. In Christ alone there is salvation.

This position – Christianity *versus* all other beliefs – is tempting. It heightens the emotional drama of conversion, and helps to give a strong grounding to individual and community identity. The problem is that this comes at a price: the price of denying or restricting God's presence in creation. It becomes easy to forget that God's first and highest gift – of existence itself – is a universal one. There is no warrant for claiming that this gift is entirely destroyed or withdrawn. What theologians sometimes call 'general' revelation is not of a wholly different and inferior kind from the 'special' revelation of distinctive Christian teaching.

God's encounter with us comes in and through the history of a people, the changing community of church, the fragile matter of the sacraments, the voice of preaching which is always finding new dialects and accents. 'Special' revelation is rooted in the original gift of creation, and always mediated through our embodied, imperfect, contextualized modes of human communication.

Surely this is unavoidable if we claim to believe in the Word made flesh, the incarnation of God's encounter with us in Christ? God does not suddenly set aside time, language, matter and change, in order to speak with a voice of timeless, immediate and self-evident certainty. God does not abolish the created world to transport eternal truths directly into our souls. Christian revelation is fleshly, particular, and always inviting new interpretation, new responses, new ways of proclamation. Our grasp of revelation is always limited. How else could it be if we are to preserve God's transcendence and the dignity of God's creation? That does not lessen its challenge, because only as incarnate truth can it touch and transform people's lives with an otherness which is not of our making.

3

Jesus and the Kingdom

The Hope of Humanity

Incarnate truth: that is the nub of Christian inclusivity. That is where time and eternity touch, where each resonates with the other's difference.

If this provides us with a general orientation in understanding the kind of communication, the kind of truth that Christian revelation is, what about the specific life and ministry of Jesus of Nazareth? Surely here we find a basic test for theology. Can we do justice to the particular history and impact of Jesus, without abandoning our starting point, our exploration of our basic human experience of being in the world?

In fact, we have already begun to do this. The doctrines of creation and fall offer a way into reading our human drama in terms of gift and loss, promise and betrayal. We are not one-dimensional beings, merely pre-programmed (by design or evolution) to accept our lot. Alongside our common humanity we sense, in some initially indistinct way, that life could be so much better than it is. We may be appalled by human suffering. We may look at others and wonder why we cannot enjoy the same success and happiness. We may experience injustice, or feel angered by injustice in the world around us. There are innumerable reasons to feel dissatisfied with who we are and the way humans behave.

But how does this dissatisfaction arise? Our unhappiness with present circumstances occurs because we have within us a vision of a better future. This vision may be flawed and incomplete. We may not be able to describe the mechanisms and process that would bring about our vision. But a conviction lies deeply seated within us that this is not 'as good as it gets'. We possess the awareness of possibilities of a greater well-being. This is true even if we have given up hope of any improvement, or have become utterly fatalistic about human progress. This fatalism is not a denial of the reality of a more perfect state, but the belief that we will never reach it.

In different ways, philosophy has tried to account for our common human experience of dissatisfaction. Plato suggested that we have within us innate knowledge of perfection that enables us to see the imperfections in human affairs. We get unhappy when we compare what we see in life with the perfect picture in our minds of how it should be. This innate knowledge gets obscured by bad habits of thinking and behaviour. So we must be educated to recover our inner awareness of perfection. Marx, taking a rather different tack, argued that we experience 'alienation': a sense of being cut off from a proper relationship with the processes of production that ensure our survival. Deep within us we somehow know how it ought to be, and we just don't feel at ease, physically or mentally, until the proper economic order (mode of production) has been achieved. Descartes, taking Plato's line a stage further, said that our awareness of the world's imperfection proved the existence of God, because only a 'perfect being' could have planted in our minds ideas of a perfect world. The Enlightenment philosophers and historians argued that we could use our reason to work out what a perfect world would look like. The existentialists wrote about our experience of 'inauthenticity' and 'uprootedness'. And so on.

These various arguments have their supporters and detractors. The point of interest here is not the list of possible answers, but the general agreement about the validity of the issue: we dream of something better. The question of what to do with these dreams is part of our human dilemma. We are aware in ourselves that we are always capable of more than we actually achieve. There always seems to be a more perfect version of ourselves, that we could become if only we knew how.

Animals, apparently, do not hope for a better life or make plans for an improved future. Living within the horizon of the present, they do not ask whether tomorrow could be any better than today. The improvement impulse appears to be a unique feature of the human experience. In other words, 'hope' is integral to what it means to be human. Nowhere is this hope more powerful than among the world's oppressed and excluded, who are more desperate than the rest of us to see some improvement in their affairs. It is a hope that empowers courage and vision in movements of liberation. A hope that breaks through the established boundaries of the existing social 'order' to make possible new ways of life.

Judeo-Christian thinking has taken the issue of a better future with great seriousness. The Old Testament prophets built their careers on proclaiming the reality of an improved social order: economic justice, international peace, right conduct in business, honesty, compassion for the needy, hospitality for the stranger and respect for all people. It is one of the most persistent and prominent Old Testament themes: theological reality is completely interwoven with an ethic of social improvement. And when the visions of the prophets wore thin, a new generation of apocalyptic writers took up the baton, imagining that God would have to bring about a world-catastrophe before human affairs could be set right.

There is both confirmation and challenge here for our basic human hope. Confirmation, because the prophets and visionaries of scripture do not simply abandon the world to its fate or recommend a spiritualized, heavenly paradise. They are not defeatists or escapists. Their words take up the longings of oppressed humanity.

However, there is also challenge, because the prophets offer a developing critique of the way those same longings become a mask for more sinister ends. So we find side by side in scripture the most bitter denunciations of enemies and the desire for vengeance upon them; *and* a radically different vision, in which the whole distinction between friend and enemy breaks down.

We might think of Abraham, receiving sustenance and blessing from the pagan priest-king Melchizedek; of Ruth, the foreigner, attaching herself to Naomi and to Naomi's God; of Jonah, compelled by God to offer the chance for penitence and mercy to the gentiles of Nineveh, when the prophet would have preferred to see them struck down for their sins. There is the recognition that Israel's role is to be a servant to the world, a light to the nations – nations in which God is also at work. There is a questioning of the role played by sacrifice in the religious cult. Perhaps other matters – justice, mercy, protection for the stranger and the vulnerable – should carry more weight: 'I desire steadfast love and not sacrifice' (Hosea 6:6).

Human longing for improvement easily becomes a desire for me and my group to emerge triumphant. The Old Testament performs a rich and challenging dialogue with this form of hope. Through the creative tensions of its stories and laws, which can't be reduced to simplistic slogans, we find a different hope coming to birth.

At the heart of much Old Testament prophetic and apocalyptic literature is the idea of a messiah: a divinely appointed leader who would lead the Jewish people, as Moses did, towards a better future. Messianic thinking plugged directly into the basic human desire for social improvement. However, alongside the dreams that a new, idealized King David would restore Israel's empire and defeat their foes, another story starts to be heard.

For one thing, the identity of the messiah was inextricably linked with the concerns of the oppressed and marginalized. The messiah would be a saviour of the excluded, gathering up 'the lost', lifting the 'yoke' from the downtrodden, and providing justice for the poor. Part of the role of the messiah, then, was to undo the effects of human exclusions and to recover the primordial state of inclusive creation.

There is more: in later chapters of the book of Isaiah (probably written in the sixth century BC), an extraordinary suggestion is made: that the figure who brings salvation to the people will not just be a victorious military leader, but will be a suffering servant, a vulnerable human being who takes on himself the pain and punishment of the people. The suffering servant absorbs the anger and hate which fuels the cycle of resentment and revenge. Only thus is hope for a new world justified.

Of course, with centuries of Christian hindsight, it is very easy to read those scattered references as a direct link with Jesus. Honesty compels us to admit two things. First, the way Jesus' story was told by the early Christians was consciously or unconsciously shaped by the suffering servant passages, so it is not altogether surprising that we see connections. Secondly, there is still much scholarly debate about the interpretation of the idea in its original context. Did it refer to a messiah-like figure, to the prophet, to the nation of Israel as a whole?

In general terms, however, we maintain that the witness of the Jewish scriptures points beyond narrowly ethnocentric, nationalistic and militaristic forms of hope and messiahship. It is in this context we should read the New Testament accounts of the ministry of Jesus. Jesus' identity is emphatically messianic, or 'Christological', and the process of understanding the nature of Jesus' messianic identity is a major theme in the Gospels – but what that means only emerges through the richness of the stories, and the radical nature of Jesus' teaching and actions.

The Open-Ended Gospel

Each of the four Gospels is, in a different way, an answer to the question that Jesus himself poses to Peter: 'Who do you say I am?' Matthew offers us a picture of Jesus as a messianic teacher, asking for faithful obedience by his followers. Mark offers us an edgy, secretive Messiah, who reveals his identity erratically to a confused band of disciples. Luke portrays Jesus as a social prophet with a humanitarian message. John shows us a cosmic Messiah who appears from the time before time, revealing himself in bold signs and gestures.

From the very beginning, then, at the fountainhead of Christian sources, 'gospel truth' has been made up of diverse voices, stories and images. These most authoritative Christian documents do not contradict the view of revelation we have been putting forward so far. If anything, they reinforce it. In all their diversity, they show just what it means for God to be made known in time, body and sign.

Let's recall the dimensions of revelation we identified earlier. First, the God revealed in Jesus enters time and history, rather than bypassing them. Jesus is born in a specific place and time, a child of Israel. He is a Jew, heir to the history of promise and relationship carried by that people. He is a Galilean, a provincial, who speaks with a particular tongue and accent. He is lower class, a joiner's son, though of dubious parentage. He lives under occupation in a land long fought over by military empires. In short, there is no way of understanding Jesus which does not take seriously his rootedness in the time and culture of his day.

As we have insisted, this is not a barrier to revelation. It is the condition for all meaningful communication. It is as a real human being, with a unique story and voice, that Jesus can engage with other stories and voices. God works in and through our humanity, not by abolishing it. The Christian claim is a radicalization of this general truth: that God commits Godself *wholly* to this means of sharing and touching our life. The incarnation is not an unfortunate interlude, after which God goes back to proclaiming timeless rules and truths from on high. This is the paradox we hold to: that God is always and everywhere (exclusively!) the inclusive, human God of Jesus Christ. It is in this light that his Messiahship must be understood: as the establishment of a new, open, humane relationship with God, in which mercy and justice walk hand in hand.

The question of Jesus' identity is not answered conclusively in the Gospels, although we are provided with the resources necessary to work on our own 'answer' – our own lived response to what we are shown. The fact that the Gospels do not 'fix' Jesus' identity in dogmatic formulae is hugely important. The Gospels open up debate about Jesus rather than closing it down. This has given the Church one of its main sources of energy, because each new generation – indeed each new Christian – must engage in faith as exploration. The truth about Jesus is not handed down from the heavens, but must be worked through a process of enquiry, interpretation and debate.

Secondly, the God revealed in Jesus is made known through story, touch, eating, drinking, friendship. In other words, this is a holistic revelation. As John Dominic Crossan puts it, 'miracle and parable, healing and eating, were calculated to force individuals into unmediated physical and spiritual contact with God and unmediated physical and spiritual contact with one another'.[1] And this is a key factor in understanding why Christians came to associate Jesus' message and his person so closely. Jesus embodies the coming kingdom or reign of God. He brings it close to people, and calls communities together which begin to live it out. He does not simply teach great moral truths and leave people to strive after them. Nor does he come as the general of an army, marshalling his troops, sacrificing them if necessary for the goal of victory. No, Jesus creates saving relationships with people, in which God desires their good, not simply their submission to divine law and command. Jesus offers healing from within the heart of the human situation.

This is another dimension of what it means to believe in incarnate truth. According to one of the maxims of the early church theologians, 'what is not assumed is not healed'. In other words, God is not about a spiritual rescue mission which saves our disembodied souls and leaves our bodies and nature to go to the wall. God is wholeheartedly committed to the whole person, and to answering the longing of creation itself for liberation (see Romans 8). Nothing is too base to be caught up in this creative, saving love. In this sense, God remains the 'jealous God' of the Old Testament. God wants everything to be reconciled, fulfilled and bursting with life.

Thirdly, this all means that the God revealed in Jesus is not a God who can be pinned down in neat but abstract definitions. The teasing question Jesus poses to his disciples, 'Who do you say that I am?', his refusal to play the game of proving where his authority comes from – these episodes witness to how Jesus resists the self-serving preconceptions of others. Those preconceptions are based on anxiety, and a corresponding demand for certainty, order and control. Jesus is a subversive figure, who transgresses the boundaries of purity and respectability, and even upsets the tables in the temple itself. Ultimately, his followers have to learn who he is only through the ending of all certainty, that breaking down of all human plans and ideologies that is represented by the cross and the resurrection.

This open-endedness of Jesus' identity is potentially dangerous to the Church as an institution. So the Church has in various ways tried to close down the debate about Jesus. The Church has tried to compensate for the lack of doctrinal certainty in the New Testament by providing various creeds that attempt to nail down the fluid and complex revelation of scripture. Creeds can be religiously useful as a foil to debate, or as stepping stones to a more exploratory faith. But we need to remember that creeds can also function to exclude, shutting down discussion and ruling certain questions, or certain conversational partners, to be illegitimate.

It is easy to forget that the process of putting the creeds together was itself a historical and human one, full of debates and politics. Their eventual form, for all the anathemas pronounced on heretics, could actually be seen as a way of trying to keep the broadest spectrum of Christian faith alive. Creeds, after all, are not definitions. They are summaries of larger stories, guides to reading those stories without trying to dispel all mystery from them, or forcing them into a narrow ideological explanation. Seen in this perspective, we have been wrong to see the creeds as barriers to further conversations. Perhaps it is better to think of them as fences keeping open a space for exploration.

Having said this, it is still the case that creeds are too often used as weapons of a defensive 'orthodoxy'. It is important to remember, therefore, that the original scriptural revelation of 'who Jesus is' is not narrowly credal or even doctrinal, but nar-

rative and poetic. We are offered scenes, stories, cameos, metaphors and images. But search as we may, there is precious little
that can be construed as doctrine. The effect of this is to make
Jesus a radically inclusive figure, because the question of his
identity invites our participation, *whoever we are*, in the forma-
tion of answers.

The implications of this are not always well understood (and
perhaps partly because the Church has not encouraged us to
understand), but the Church does not 'own' the true answer to
the question of Jesus' identity. A Muslim or Jew, Hindu or atheist can stake as much claim to an understanding of Jesus' identity as any Pope or Archbishop. Having said that, the claims of the
churches to have a better understanding of Jesus carry a particular weight, and arguments can be offered of various kinds to say
that the Church has been granted privileged insight into Jesus.
But this does not exclude the insights that others might bring to
the discussion. The Church does not have property rights over
Jesus, indeed it does not even 'possess' the Christian scriptures.

So when we speak about Christology, that's to say the messianic
identity of Jesus, we are referring not to a set of doctrines, but
to a field of exploration and enquiry. Anyone, potentially, is included in this enquiry. A true Church – if such a thing will ever
exist – should allow rights of speech to everyone in the debate
about Jesus. The true Church really would be that inclusive. This
inclusion is predicated upon a fundamental faith that Christians
have nothing to fear from open enquiry and that Jesus does not
need 'protecting' from awkward questions. This is a radical faith
in Jesus himself, a faith that liberates the Church from the heresy
that God is too weak to defend himself.

Jesus' Open Table

When we look with an open mind at the portrayal of Jesus in the Gospels, we notice that he has very little interest in religious organizations and their rules. When he does speak of religion, it is generally to point out its dangers or to offer blistering critique. Jesus hardly mentions the idea of 'church' at all – indeed the word 'church' does not appear in three of the four Gospels. Instead Jesus speaks repeatedly about his mission to announce the arrival of what he calls 'the kingdom of God'. This new kingdom is a new social order. And, as Jesus explains, this new social order places great emphasis upon 'inclusion'.

Although there are indications in the Gospels that Jesus thought of himself as a purely Jewish messiah and that the kingdom would only be for Jews, Jesus' predominant concerns are inclusive. He says (Luke 4) that his 'good news' will reach out to those at every social margin: good news for the poor, the captive, the blind, and the oppressed. Jesus keeps the company of the despised sections of society: 'publicans', tax collectors, Samaritans and prostitutes. One of the defining features of Jesus' ministry is his friendship with women and the absence in his teaching of any pejoratives about women. He mixes with lepers and he challenges the idea that anyone can be ritually 'unclean'.

We are instructed not to judge others and to practise an ethic of indiscriminate acceptance. Jesus criticizes employment practices that are likely to lead to hardship for employees, and he preaches debt-forgiveness. He uses the example of a Samaritan to illustrate how good Jews ought to behave (and from whom they should be prepared to *receive* mercy and truth). He says that everyone from the highways and byways will be welcome to eat with him in his kingdom. Special privileges will come to the humble, but the rich will struggle to find a place in the new kingdom. Jesus says that the all-important central ethic of love must transcend family and tribal bonds, reaching out even to one's enemies. Wherever we look, Jesus' teaching is shot through with values of inclusion.

Jesus' inclusive ideal is perhaps best captured in his image of the eschatological feast. The fulfilment of his kingdom will be like a vast meal with a place for everyone at table. The feast will not include those who have neglected their neighbours in need, but there are no categorical exclusions on the grounds of gender, divorce, race, sexual orientation or any physical differences. The inheritors of the kingdom will be those who hear his word and keep it: in other words, the future belongs to those who practise the inclusive ethics of the kingdom.

It is telling that the Dead Sea Scrolls reveal an alternative vision of 'perfect' human community among the Essene sect. The Essenes saw themselves as a messianic elite, a 'house of holiness'. They defined themselves by their exclusiveness, and they were obsessed with hierarchies, purity and protocols. Their view of perfect community was a stratified theocracy which could only come about once their foes had been destroyed. The priests would act as generals and there would be no mercy for the 'wicked flesh' of their enemies. Unlike Jesus' open feast, places at the Essene banquet were strictly reserved for insiders. Their imagined banquet specifically excludes 'any one halt or blind or lame, or a man in whose body is a permanent defect, or a man affected by an impurity of his flesh'.[2] Such glimpses of Essene religion throw into relief the inclusive and counter-cultural character of Jesus' teaching about ideal community.

Intimations of this feast appear throughout the Gospels. Jesus, we are told, is quite different from John the Baptist because he 'comes eating and drinking', showing that the sharing of meals is a distinctive feature of Jesus' ministry. Ched Myers has argued that Jesus' feeding miracles – of the 4,000 and 5,000 – are of particular significance because they function as political gestures, asserting a new kingdom economy of gift, sharing and reciprocity.[3] Jesus is famously criticized by religious purists for keeping the wrong kind of company at his table, showing that he cared nothing for the politics of social exclusion and stigmatization. And at the Last Supper Jesus insists on feeding Judas personally, including him in the table fellowship of the disciples even at the moment he is betraying them. After the resurrection Jesus enjoys a number of meals with the apostles, showing that communal 'bread fellowship' can thrive even on the far side of violence and betrayal. 'The feast' is a metaphor for non-violent, forgiving, compassionate community. The happening of this feast is a sign of the 'new creation' and the rediscovery of the radical inclusion of our divine creation.

What, though, of that text so often quoted by conservatives: 'I am the way, the truth and the life. No one comes to the Father except through me' (John 14)? Surely this says loud and clear that salvation is exclusive to followers of Jesus. On one reading it certainly does. But if we read this text in the light of Jesus' more general ethic of inclusion, the text takes a quite different meaning. If Jesus' 'way' is the path of a generous and non-judgemental love, then the path to the Father is not narrow dogmatism but an inclusive ethics. So this is not a text directed against peoples of other faiths or no faith at all, but a warning to those who would adopt any other path than that shown by the personal example of Jesus. It returns us to the creative tension of our claim that inclusion is *the* truth. The only way to walk with this God is through letting our excluding barriers fall.

We may reasonably ask, however, whether this 'inclusive messiah' isn't just another dogma. There is certainly a constant risk that a radical-inclusive understanding of Jesus will end up offering itself as another dogmatic certainty. But this need not be the case. The 'inclusive' understanding of Jesus simply has the status of an interpretation that must defend itself in the debate about Jesus' identity. This is the same for every 'version' of Jesus. Just don't expect those defending an 'inclusive messiah' to be lacking in vigour and conviction. We are laying claim to the very heart and soul of the Christian message and intend to argue our case forcefully.

4

Jesus and the Cross

Just a Good Person?

The most powerful and persuasive dimension to Jesus' teaching is that he acted out the inclusive ethics even to the point of death. The crucifixion shows Jesus' non-violent, forgiving and non-judgemental ethics at work in the most challenging circumstances.

To speak of Jesus' death 'living out' or 'embodying' an ethic might appear to do scant justice to traditional Christian understandings of the cross. The issue is this: if Jesus is no more than a good man, or even a divine example of how to lead a good life, then his death can make no objective difference to the world. It doesn't have any material effect on our relationship with God. It's worth teasing this out a little more, because of the deep impact it can have on our understanding of what God is like, and how God is known to us.

Many people would affirm that Jesus was a 'good' person, a prophet, a teacher of abiding values. On this view, his death shows his commitment to those values to the end. It also represents the tragic end of an innocent man unjustly persecuted. The problem for Christianity is that none of this appears to put Jesus in a special category. We can find plenty of inspiring people throughout history, and plenty who suffered innocently and died at the hands of violent opponents. Jesus may be interesting, inspiring, even unique – but he remains merely an example of how to lead a good life.

This falls far short of the claims Christians have made about Jesus: that he is the one who effectively reconciles us to God, the one who actually overcomes the division that exists between us and God. He is more than a pointing finger, showing us the way to walk – he *is* that way, the one who carries us where we cannot go ourselves. If this is lost, we also lose any sense of Jesus being a saviour, and of the undeserved grace of God at work through him. Christianity becomes debased into a moralistic religion of works, in which it is up to us to be 'good', and in which we create and project our own ideas of what that goodness consists of. All the time, our fundamental alienation from God, each other and ourselves remains untouched.

This critique can also be applied to some more explicitly Christian approaches to understanding Jesus' death. A popular notion – forged particularly out of the experience of the devastating wars and genocides of the last century – has refused to play down the divine nature of Jesus, but has used this to claim that, in him, God suffers *alongside* humanity. God is not a distant, unmoved mover, but one who assumes humanity in order to go to the very depths of human experience in solidarity with those who are persecuted, abused and in pain.

It is a powerful image, summed up in the title (derived from Luther) of Jürgen Moltmann's striking work *The Crucified God*. In many ways, it represents a radical departure from the classical Greek idea of God, so influential in Christian theology. According to this, God, being perfect, must remain impassible. This means God cannot be affected by change of any kind, including suffering and death. Moltmann and others have sought to uphold what they see as a more distinctively Christian revelation of God humbling himself to share in our humanity, even to death.

As we have mentioned, this approach also has its critics. The risk is that the crucified God 'shares our pain' but doesn't actually *do* anything to change our situation. We are offered comfort, but nothing more. A divine Jesus who suffers with us is, in the final reckoning, little better than the human Jesus who is merely a good teacher, wrongly killed. Each can simply be the reflection of human ideas of goodness or compassion which, for all their poetry and attractiveness, are graceless and powerless to change the world. We are left hanging on the cross of our broken existence.

Despite the objections, it is worth asking why these contemporary approaches have had such a big influence. There is certainly a positive attempt to do justice to the reality of suffering in Jesus' life, and to understand how this is relevant to our individual and collective experiences of devastation and disaster. But there has also been a reaction against some of the implications of past theological accounts of Jesus' death. Why?

Limiting God: Flawed Theories of the Cross

The New Testament contains a number of images and metaphors which articulate the meaning of the cross. Jesus' death is a ransom, a victory over the powers of the age, the overcoming of death, the strength and wisdom of God revealed in weakness and foolishness. It is reconciliation, solidarity and self-offering. This rich vocabulary has been preserved in scripture and celebrated in liturgy, and never reduced down to a one-sided view by the creeds of the Church.

However, over the course of the Church's history, especially since the rise of modern conservative evangelicalism, one particular way of talking about the cross has claimed dominance over all others. It is often called the penal substitution model of the atonement. It states that human beings are sinners, to the extent that they are incapable of any goodness which would be able to save them and restore their relationship with God. Moreover, the proper punishment for sin is death, because it is disobedience to the God who gives life. In this state, all we deserve is death or even eternal punishment in hell.

God wants to do something about this. God wants to save us, because he is merciful. But he is also a God of justice and cannot abandon his own nature. His holiness means he cannot bear to be in the presence of sin. His righteousness demands that sin cannot simply be ignored. God can't let us off and accept us as we are, without the price of sin being paid. Therefore, Jesus, who is both God and man, takes our place, takes the punishment for sin on himself. He pays the price for sin with his blood. He is the perfect sacrifice (being without sin himself), who alone can suffer in our place.

In many ways, this is a deeply moving *story* of a God who takes upon himself all the consequences of evil, and who stands between us and destruction. But when it is treated as more than a suggestive narrative, when it is elevated to the level of *explanation*, it is seriously flawed.

For one thing, it depends on certain assumptions about God, which must be called into question by Jesus' own ministry. God, we are told, is so holy, he cannot bear the presence of sin. And yet Jesus is berated by the religious insiders of his day precisely because he ate with tax collectors and sinners, and allowed people considered unclean and sinful to touch him. God, we are further informed, cannot set aside his 'justice', and so must demand the price for sin is paid. But Jesus demands no price when he shares his table fellowship with others. He does indeed challenge people (especially the rich) to change their life. But this is not set as a condition for approaching him. Rather, it is the very openness of his invitation which seems to be the first step which enables people to change. Think of Zacchaeus in Luke 19, who is first invited to be with Jesus, and *then* offers to transform his life. Indeed, Jesus seems to suggest that God does not wait for us to find him, but actively seeks people out before they have fully repented (like the woman searching for the lost coin, or the father of the prodigal son, running to meet him on the road before the young man can offer his self-interested 'confession').

Finally, we are assured that human beings are so utterly corrupted by sin that they can make no approach to God. But the Gospels show many people seeking Jesus out, knowing their need of healing and longing for connection. They may have mixed motives, they may need to overcome the self-interested and idolatrous religious ideas they bring with them, but there is no suggestion that these people are so entirely depraved as to make their coming to Jesus worthless. On the contrary, his response is often to say to those he heals 'Your faith has made you well.' The implication is that these people have faith *before* they meet him.

The penal substitution theory is too mechanistic, too legalistic to reflect the God of the Bible. It elevates an abstract law of justice or holiness above God's own nature. In so doing, it reflects more of human ideas of religion, based on sacrifice and deals done with the gods, than it does of Christian revelation. God becomes trapped by his own rigour, unable to forgive without exacting punishment. The irony is that this theory seems to put God at a lower moral level than (depraved) humanity!

A further difficulty with the penal theory is that it easily devalues the rest of Jesus' ministry. If all that was required for our salvation was a substitute sacrifice, then why didn't Jesus just go straight to the cross and get the job done? The reason, surely, is that it was Jesus' complete life that effected salvation: his birth, ministry, passion and resurrection. It is a mistake to focus our theology of salvation exclusively on the three hours of the crucifixion. This risks turning the incarnation and ministry of Jesus into a mere warm-up to the main action. A more rounded and complete theology of the atonement will show how Jesus' entire life was a salvific act.

The great second-century theologian Irenaeus made just this point, arguing that Jesus hallowed every stage of human life, deepening it and leading it to God. Irenaeus certainly did not water down the scope of salvation. Out of love, God in Christ embraces our whole humanity and unites it to the divine heart: 'Our Lord Jesus Christ, the Word of God, in his boundless love, became what we are that he might make us what he himself is.' He is able to make this claim, because he does not buy into the idea that humanity is utterly lost. For Irenaeus, we are on a journey of growth into maturity, a journey begun in creation, misdirected by sin, and perfected in Christ. Again we are reminded not to divorce our ideas of salvation and atonement from the original gift and ongoing blessing of creation.

In the light of this, we shouldn't be too dismissive when Christians and others have sought alternative ways of telling the story, focusing on the elements of human compassion and courage. If the New Testament itself shows the early Christian communities and writers in a vibrant and diverse process of exploration, we too need to be able to 'try out' a range of images and narratives, to see how they match with life as it is given to us. Just as there isn't only one Gospel, so there will never be one and only one way of defining what the cross means.

We can see here a good example of the distinctive character of inclusive theology. The instincts of the inclusive theologian are to explore new possibilities and interpretations, rather than to defend one dogmatic version to the bitter end. This is because inclusive theology is more concerned with exploring the truth than defending the currently fashionable version of 'orthodoxy'. In the process, we rediscover that the real Christian tradition is alive and well, and full of alternatives to our prevailing myopia.

The Cross and the End of Sacrifice

The history of the theology of the atonement shows that the Church has not had one single consistent theory of the cross. The early ransom and victory theories were replaced after 1,000 years by Anselm's substitution theory, which offered a completely different version of events. The ransom and victory theories showed a heroic Christ fighting, or outwitting, the forces of evil and death. The substitution theory showed Jesus meekly submitting to the law of his Father. These theories could hardly be more different. And that is not to mention the powerful strand represented by Irenaeus and others, for whom it is Jesus' whole humanity that enables us to continue our growth towards God-given maturity.

This difference is only a problem if we insist on seeing theology as a static system of knowledge that must be slavishly passed down the generations. There is no scope here for new knowledge, or for more than one mode of expression. If on the other hand we see theology as dynamic knowledge, responding to new ideas and criticism, then the development of atonement theology is evidence of the vitality of the Church's thinking. If we imagine that theology were a form of music, then the neo-orthodox view is that every generation should play the same tunes. The inclusive theologian, by contrast, is always interested to see what other kinds of music are possible.

This being said, we still need to ask: what does Jesus' death *do*, what new reality does it cause to break into ours, so that we are not just imposing our ready-made ideas of goodness and compassion on him? One answer is inspired by the seminal work of René Girard. It contends that, rather than seeing Jesus' death as a sacrifice, or literally paying the price for sin, we should see it as the *end of sacrifice*, denying that there is any price that needs to be paid for our acceptance.

This is a powerful theme in Christian scripture and tradition. Jesus' death, once and for all, was seen to put a stop to the need to make repeated sacrifices to appease God. However, Girard's suggestion is not just that Jesus' death was the sacrifice to end all others, but that it showed us how wrong and destructive the whole notion of a religion based on sacrifice is. Put simply, Girard claims that there is a basic dynamic of human desire, in which we learn what is desirable from one another, and then become locked in deadly competition to possess our objects. The futility of this situation is resolved when we decide to load our frustration and guilt on to a representative figure, who is offered up or excluded (like the biblical scapegoat), bearing the cost of our violent confrontation, while (temporarily) uniting us and helping us overcome our differences.

Girard is describing a powerful element in human society, but it's one we see at work in everyday life. The 'weird' kids in the schoolyard become the butt of everyone else's ridicule, a way of uniting the rest of the kids in common cause. The asylum seeker becomes the hate figure, the symbol of an impurity that is corrupting 'our' way of life. The mature single mum who goes to university is labelled a snob, who thinks she is better than her peers. Gays, lesbians, bisexuals and the transgendered are ridiculed and abominated because they do not abide by the straight norm. These people become the scapegoats, over against whom communities define themselves in symbolic and actual acts of exclusion and violence.

On the cross, Jesus takes the place of the scapegoat, and stands with the excluded. In doing so he *is* being true to his teaching. Not just by suffering for what's right, but in challenging the means by which we come up with ideas of right and wrong in the first place. He has called a community together from his practice of open table fellowship, a community which is supposed to be free from reactionary vengefulness, exclusion and tyrannical power. Now he calls that community to be true to him even as the criminal subversive, the scapegoat, the one cursed and outcast by a shameful death imposed upon him by the imperial powers.

What is crucial to see here is that the community Jesus has called breaks apart in the face of this challenge. Most of his followers betray, deny and abandon him, apart from the women who risk their reputations to tend his body and tomb. The cross shows that our most noble efforts at personal and political relationship have to be radically transformed by an encounter with this love that does not let the fear of death and shame define our reality. In proclaiming Jesus as Lord, the early Christians were registering the aftershock of their experience that it was the crucified one who showed them what is real. The ultimate or deepest reality is that of reconciling, boundary-crossing love.

Losing Control: The Cost of Inclusion

The claim that Jesus is divine does not begin with speculations about his metaphysical make-up, but here, with the shattering experience of the cross that he shows us what really matters and takes us to a place where we can begin to live it out. These first followers believed that Jesus reigns, invites and forgives even as he hangs on the cross. They believed it so much they refused to take part in the imperial cult, serve in its armies or play in its gladiatorial circuses of cruelty. And that was a huge challenge to the violent imperial political system under which they lived, and to all the notions of religion which defined communities by sacrifice, scapegoating and exclusion.

The Christian Church that began to grow after Jesus' death only did so out of the rubble of its own attempts to control and define reality according to inherited ideas of power and purity. It bears witness to the fact that Jesus' death is inseparable from the creation of a new sort of human community. But it also bears witness to its inability to be that community, except in fragile and broken ways. It has to point beyond itself, because Jesus does not come to create a church as another in-group over against everyone else, but to show what the whole business of being human is and can be about. If the Church is a faithful witness to Christ, it has to practise his open and inclusive fellowship *and* it has to recognize and celebrate the fact that people are being caught up in that commonality beyond its own limited borders and restricted imagination. Whenever the Church proclaims the Lord's death, it announces its own provisionality, and it rejoices in that. A church which asserts itself as the goal of God's mission, the definer of God's truth or the ruler of God's people is falling into the old compulsions which have always enslaved people.

Many accounts of differences in the churches seem to suggest that we have to make a choice between two basic directions. The first option is that we defend a form of Christianity which is distinctive, demanding and which stands against many of the cultural trends in our society. The second is that Christians adopt a more conciliatory approach to the surrounding world, recognizing God's presence within it, learning from it and seeking points of contact between world and Church. And it is assumed that these two approaches are mutually incompatible.

Nonsense. The inclusiveness of the Church is precisely what makes it a demanding, counter-cultural presence in the world. The Church bears witness to the good news that tribalism, militarism and consumerism do not have the last word upon us, because all these forms of securing human identity are at bottom violent, grasping and anxious. The kind of community opened up by Jesus and marked with the sign of the cross offers a place for unlearning this violence and fear, and living in different kinds of personal and political relationship. If the community turns inward, if it starts proclaiming itself as the goal of salvation and the bastion of certainty, then it is turning its back on the way of Christ. It is mimicking the powers of the world, be they political, corporate or military. It is by living an inclusive and reconciling way that the Church can bear witness, with others, to the radical challenge that Jesus embodies.

The centrality of the cross makes this inescapable. The cross is a decisive break with religions of control and exclusion and purity. It is the stumbling block for all our attempts to create a God we want, whether that means a God of domination who takes from us the responsibility and anxiety of living as free human beings, or a God of ethereal spirituality who helps us escape from the harshness of life. Dictatorships and capitalism have little to fear from such convenient deities. The crucified Jesus shows us the God who is real and inconvenient: a God of the whole of life, not just a private inner sanctuary; a God of non-violence and reconciliation, not one who blesses the armies of the world; a God who offers food without price, not another brand name.

This has been obscured by those Christian theories of the atonement which have perpetuated the idea that God demands violence in order to forgive, to preserve his purity and show his power. Our contention is that these theories, far from ensuring the distinctiveness of Christianity, have only succeeded in echoing the world's love affair with violence as a means of settling disputes and bringing people together. In contrast, we affirm the cross as God's protest against violence and the reopening of other possibilities for community and justice.

So Jesus *is* a good man living out his teaching to the bitter end. *But* that teaching is not mere information or morals. It is a way of living, in which we can be caught up with others and shaken enough to question and change our destructive patterns of behaviour. It is not just another disciplinary voice telling us to try harder, but a way of grace into which we are invited.

Jesus *is* the one who shows us God's solidarity and compassion. *But* that only bears fruit in forms of human relationship which are empowered to resist the deadening forces of oppression, poverty and division. God does not helplessly share our pain, but creates a new context for us to resist the forces that dehumanize us.

In other words, we can see the grace of God at work in the cross, but not if it is something done to us, as passive recipients. Jesus called people to lose their lives to find them, and Paul speaks of Christians sharing in the death and resurrection of Christ. Revelation is not a mechanical event 'out there' or a downloading of new information from 'up there'. It is an encounter, an invitation, a coming back to life in the company of others: he 'became what we are that he might make us what he himself is'.

It is worth dwelling on this intimate connection between life and death in the Christian tradition. Feminist writers and others have questioned the role the crucifixion plays in Christian piety, because it seems to recommend the kind of self-denial and self-sacrifice which is anything but liberating for those who need to rediscover their own worth. But Paul and Jesus speak of losing or dying to false forms of identity, in which the love of God, neighbour and oneself are denied. The costliness of this cannot be underestimated, but it must never be identified with passive submission to abuse and oppression. That hardly sounds like the life Jesus lived, and Paul sought to follow! Jesus did not hold back in challenging the powerful and the pious, and exposing their (and our) strategies of control. Paul offered a vision of Christians discovering a new, empowered identity in the Spirit, one which would release their gifts while setting aside the inequalities of the world. The gift and cost of discipleship is found, not in accepting the fear of death and punishment, but in the perfect love which casts out fear, and calls us to live a life which can bring us into conflict with the power games of the world (and sometimes the Church).

Death is one of the subjects which Western culture shies away from, no doubt because it cannot be accommodated in our media-led dreams of eternal youthfulness. We celebrate only firm, slim bodies, shored up by plastic surgery and smoothed by anti-ageing creams. At the same time, we try to sanitize death and isolate ourselves (particularly our children) from its presence. The dead and the dying make no economic contribution, they consume little or nothing, and they remind us that no matter what we accumulate, no matter what status we hold, we will join them. Death asks questions our secular culture finds hard to hear, let alone answer.

Christian faith calls us to face death honestly, as part of our humanity. We do not need to hide death away, or buy into the fake eternity of the cosmetics marketplace. The cross reminds us to live with death as a reality, but one which does not have the last word on who we are. It calls us to real life, flowing from the gift of creation, renewed in the ministry of Jesus and shared through the challenging hospitality of his followers. In that context, we don't have to cling to our narrow certainties and rigid structures in order to stave off death. That is the difference the cross has made and continues to make in our world.

5

Jesus and the Resurrection

The Resurrection as Living Story

If the crucifixion were the last word in the story, then Christian theology would be arrested in tragedy. We would be left frozen in a moment of stark but painful reality, staring at uncertainty, death and suffering. The Good Friday experience of facing up to human frailty is very necessary, especially in our escapist culture. But it is not enough.

Jesus' teaching about the kingdom of God contained promises about the kind of world that we might live in: promises of social equality, human fulfilment and distributive justice. At the Last Supper, Jesus reassured his followers that they would drink wine together in his 'kingdom'. The grieving were promised comfort and the famished were promised food and drink. If Good Friday is the last chapter of Jesus' life, then what happens to his inclusive agenda?

There is a theological and narrative imperative for the story of Jesus to continue after Good Friday in order that we can have some reassurance of human flourishing beyond tragedy. And the Gospels do not disappoint, supplying us with a continuation of the story: the resurrection of Jesus. Following Good Friday, the Gospel writers report 'appearances' of Jesus. These 'appearances' have the effect of galvanizing the early Church into the task of continuing Jesus' work. His followers feel that they have

Jesus' spirit with them and that they themselves are now Jesus' 'body'. Jesus does not need a body on earth because the Church will be his body, doing his will.

Quite what transpired historically at that time is unclear, and this is not the moment to offer a theory of what may have happened. It is clear that Jesus was taken for dead on Good Friday, and it is clear that the early Church enjoyed spectacular confidence and success shortly afterwards. What happened in between is not properly recoverable and must remain the subject of historical speculation.

Although it may seem a strange thing to say, the 'facts' of the resurrection have never been the key issue for Christians – although many have wasted time down that cul-de-sac. The principal issue for Christians is what the resurrection means. This question applies, whatever our theory of the facts. Even the person who thinks that the resurrection is just a piece of Christian folklore must explain what the resurrection episode means in the context of the narrative of Jesus' life as a whole. In reading the story of the resurrection – whether historically or fictionally – we need to work out what the Gospel writers are trying to tell us about Jesus.

Biblical theology in the second half of the twentieth century was dominated by the question of the historical realism of the Gospels: did the miracles happen? Was there a virgin birth? Was the resurrection a historical event? Was Jesus really the 'son of God', or was this just fanciful thinking? Theologians lined up on both sides, either writing all or parts of the story of Jesus off as first-century mythology, or feeling they had to defend its 'historical truth'. This stand-off stopped debate in its tracks. There was no common ground from which to launch continuing discussion. The liberals regarded the conservatives as naive literalists, and the conservatives thought that the liberals had given up their faith. Each regarded the other from its own citadel.

More importantly, the theological significance of the resurrection received too little attention. The meaning of the resurrection is a function of the story as a whole: it only makes sense after the crucifixion and before the beginnings of the Church. The meaning of the resurrection is not a stand-alone 'fact', but an episode within a larger narrative. This meaning is not dependent upon a prior theory about the historicity of the resurrection.

It is important that we do not turn the historicity of the Gospels into something more important than the Gospels themselves. The revelation of who Jesus is is given to us in a narrative text. The tradition of the Church has been to regard this narrative as sacred and authoritative. To treat the historical facts about Jesus as our starting point for evaluating the Gospels pushes the authority of the scriptural narrative into second place. History becomes our new authority, and scripture is transformed into the status of mere 'evidence' of the historical reality. Once 'history' becomes the measure of scripture, the truth about Jesus finds itself balanced precariously on the outcome of every new archaeological dig in Palestine, or every new theory about 'who Jesus really was'. Scripture is continually at risk of being overruled by history.

But once the story of Jesus is taken in its purity as a 'narrative' (historical or otherwise), a different cluster of questions comes into view: what is the 'truth' of this narrative? Is this narrative 'authoritative' for us in an ethical and religious way? Does this narrative inspire us? Does it transform or illuminate our understanding of life? These are the questions that we need to ask, and we can ask them with the same passion whatever our particular take on history.

Some will say that this is a cop-out and that we 'must' take a decisive view on the historical truth of the resurrection. But this is the very opposite of a cop-out: this is the recovery of scripture as scripture, the appropriation of the story of Jesus exactly as it is told to us. What we recover in a thorough-going narrative approach is *the true Jesus* released from the captivity of his empirical inquisitors. The story of Jesus can now be followed without having to stop at every turn to answer the question: 'But did this really happen?' This is immensely liberating. With a narrative approach we can own the complete story of Jesus, without having to play down or ignore the 'difficult' supernatural bits. Conservatives are also freed up from the necessity to justify the unexplainable: such as Jesus walking on water, or the ascension. What is more, the narrative approach still allows us to take history seriously. We can still have a view about the historical reality of the resurrection, indeed this view may contribute to our overall understanding of the story. But history is no longer the arbiter of scriptural truth.

It is worth pausing a moment to restate comments made in the Introduction about the nature of 'scriptural truth'. This truth is the *narrative truth* of the story in all its complexity and ambiguity. The narrative truth of Christianity is not, as John Milbank and the Radical Orthodoxy school have argued, a single, coherent myth whose identity and meaning are somehow obvious. Scripture is, rather, a complex and multi-layered textual reality in which a multitude of interpretations are possible.

The truth of scripture remains stubbornly woven into its layers of story and metaphor. Scripture cannot be reduced to its essence, or kerygma, or an abstract meaning. The only way to encounter the truth of scripture is to take the book up in one's hand and begin to interpret. The commitment to scriptural truth is, above all, a commitment to hermeneutics.

Some of the metaphors we use about the Bible can be unhelpful. We often use a vocal metaphor and refer to 'what the Bible says'. Or we imagine that the Bible is a rational consciousness that can have 'opinions' and 'points of view'. This personification of the Bible into a 'speaking book' is very natural, and we all do it – but also very misleading. The Bible doesn't have a voice and it cannot speak, hold opinions or take points of view. The Bible is a series of texts that require interpretation. The Bible is mute, more like a painting that must be gazed upon, interpreted, read and reread. The result of our labours of interpretation is not 'a voice' but 'a reading'. A reading requires a reader who must account for her interpretation, who must take responsibility for her interpretation. Listening to the imagined 'voice' of scripture carries no such responsibility, because the listener can say: 'Look: this is what I've been told.' The metaphor of speech disguises the fact that the Bible must always be subjected to a *reading*.

Scripture challenges radically any expectations we may have that the truth is an idea and that scripture is merely its container. To access the truth of scripture we must engage in an open-ended labour of interpretation, opening up an ever-changing world of interactions between the text and its audiences. Scriptural truth is not waiting somewhere within the text to be plucked out by the reader. Rather, the truth of scripture arises in the context of reading and interpretation. This is not so much a truth that exists passively, but a truth that happens dynamically in the process of reading.

Life Beyond Exclusion

So let us examine the resurrection from a narrativist perspective. We see that the truth and authority of the resurrection is tied up with the narrative necessities of the story of Jesus. The story demands the resurrection in order to reaffirm Jesus' kingdom-values on the far side of the violence and betrayals of Good Friday. The death of Jesus cuts savagely across the inclusivist vision that Jesus had been teaching in his ideas about the kingdom. The crucifixion is an ultimate act of exclusion: an exclusion from life itself. And in normal stories, this exclusion would be final.

The events before and during the death of Jesus also poison the fellowship of the disciples: Judas' betrayal, Peter's repeated denials, and the collective failure of the disciples to stand by Jesus during his ordeal – or even to stay awake at Gethsemane. Peter is left 'weeping bitterly', Judas hangs himself and the remaining disciples are traumatized with horror, guilt and grief.

At this juncture in the narrative, the resurrection – or something with equivalent power – is an emotional and social necessity. The disciples need to feel forgiven and have their faith restored again in the possibility of an inclusive and non-violent community.

The resurrection appearances of Jesus have some very important and distinctive features. First, Jesus appears in his former human body, still bearing the marks of violence. The resurrection is not a theophany, but a restoration of the solid, living and breathing person of Jesus. Secondly, Jesus uses a new form of greeting when he sees the disciples: 'Peace be with you.' This phrase is unique to the resurrection and is not spoken by Jesus before this time. Thirdly, the resurrection appearances are predominantly associated with the sharing of meals: a meal at Emmaus, a meal by the sea of Tiberias and the sharing of food in Jerusalem.

The reappearance of Jesus in his own created body shows that the resurrection is not the inauguration of a new era, but the restoration of the original created order. The resurrection does not 'improve' creation, trump it with something better, or replace it with another kind of existence. The resurrection reinstates the created human body after it has been abused, assaulted and left to die. So the resurrection life is not so much 'new life' as 'renewed life'. In this way the resurrection is the most radical affirmation of the inclusive and created order.

But it is not only the broken body that needs mending. The community of the disciples has been disfigured by conspiracy, betrayal and cowardice. After Jesus' death, they are frightened and guilty. They do not know whether Jesus' resurrection will mean forgiveness or punishment. The disciples are in need of reconciliation, and this is why the resurrected Jesus introduces himself with words of benediction: 'Peace be with you.' This greeting reassures the disciples that the resurrection does not mean recrimination and revenge. The resurrection experience is, for the disciples, not only the reaffirmation of Jesus' created body but the healing of their broken communion.

More significantly, Jesus restores the broken table fellowship of the disciples by sharing meals with them. This is a real and symbolic reinstatement of friendship, a sign to them that their former communion has not been lost, and that the eschatological feast is not a vain hope. The resurrection meals are symbolic models of community based upon sharing, forgiveness and non-violence. It is this vision of community that the disciples tried to carry forward as they established the Church.

This vision is expansive and inclusive. Jesus does not say that anyone should be categorically excluded from the Church, and he has nothing whatsoever to say about the categories of people suitable to serve as leaders. Instead, Jesus leaves behind an ethos: the enduring memory of feeling forgiven, included and affirmed. The early Church struggled to understand how this inclusive community should be structured. And part of the history of the early Church that we read in the New Testament is the story of the Church's failure to realize Jesus' inclusive and non-judgemental ethics. There were crises and disputes, blind alleys and failed missions, but the Church could always draw upon the memory of a resurrection that included them. Despite everything, Jesus accepted them and forgave them.

6

The Inclusive Church

A Community of Witness

The Church, then, has to be understood in the context we have outlined so far. Put negatively, the Church is not the goal of God's creative process. Nor is it the sole context in which God can be encountered and known. The absurdly inflated claims made for the role and importance of the Church in some recent theology make no sense if the basic thrust of an inclusive theology is accepted. They represent a self-defeating inward turn on the part of theologians no longer able to command influence in the public arena.

Freed from the unreal and idolatrous expectation that the Church is and can be the exclusive vehicle for God's presence in the world, its positive potential can unfold. It is a living, embodied community of witness to the gift of creation, the unity of humankind and the invitation to share in God's life which is at the heart of Jesus' ministry, death and resurrection.

Thus, an inclusive approach by no stretch of the imagination surrenders the distinctive identity of the Church, or its rootedness in the revelation of God in creation, scripture, tradition and human experience. The Church is not there simply to baptize the surrounding culture, any more than it can turn its back on the world around it.

In order to get beyond such bleak dichotomies, it helps to reflect on why they have come into being in the first place. Part of the answer lies in the traumas which shook the Church and theology in the first half of the twentieth century. One of theology's formative narratives is heavily influenced by the career of the great Swiss thinker, Karl Barth. Barth's own development was shaped by the disastrous accommodations made by the German Protestant churches, first in their support of the Kaiser's war effort in 1914, and secondly in the subservience to Nazism offered by the so-called 'German Christian' movement in the 1930s.

Barth's furious and undoubtedly courageous response to these movements led him to an uncompromising rejection of natural theology, and of any approach to God built on the shifting, polluted sands of human experience, culture and values. Unfortunately, his influence was such that theologians since have often allowed Barth's particular reaction to set the agenda for the Church, with the result that theological trends swing between one-sided extremes. Either we have to abandon the distinctiveness of the Christian story and community, and allow it to become an uncritical religious veneer decorating secular culture; or we have to proclaim the Church as a community set over against the world, finding its identity solely in the story it tells about itself, a story that it ultimately must identify with the one that God is telling. Either assimilation, or exclusivism. These are the options that an uncritical acceptance of Barth's theology has bequeathed to us.

It is worth recalling that Barth's response was not the only possible one, however. Another theologian who – literally – spent his life's blood in fighting Nazism was Dietrich Bonhoeffer. Bonhoeffer was a complex thinker, who shared many of Barth's presuppositions at first. However, there can be little doubt that his unfinished writings were suggestive of a very dif-

85

ferent understanding of the potential for Christian dialogue with a mature secular outlook.

Indeed, a dialogical approach enjoyed a resurgence in the post-war period, when theologians sought to engage with the questions of contemporary culture. However, as the optimism surrounding economic reconstruction, technological progress and sexual liberation drifted into an era of widening inequality, the arms race, terror and AIDS, so a more pessimistic conservatism has taken centre stage in theology. It is a defensive reaction, calling the Church to retreat into its own structures and its own private language. While this approach offers a sense of security in a changing and divided world, it is as much a capitulation to cultural trends as over-optimistic forms of liberalism ever were. When theologians start demanding Christian withdrawal from the tainted activities of the secular state; or call society to return to 'traditional' family values; or attack multiculturalism for being unchristian, they are simply mimicking the moves made by conservative politicians across the world. Such conservatism refuses to tackle systems of domination and declines to engage seriously with the limits of knowledge and fluidity of identity. Worst of all, it fails to respond generously to the inclusive social movements which do offer an alternative to unrestrained capitalism and dogmatic totalitarianism.

The Unfinished Church

Much ink has been spilt on trying to number and catalogue the 'marks' of a true and valid church. An alternative approach is to accept that the Church is always a work in progress, and is neither infallible nor indefectible. In fact, as a living, embodied community of witness, one of its 'marks' should be a continual openness to reform, as new questions are asked, new challenges faced, new insights won. Those who complain that this risks compromising the Church's uniqueness are in one sense quite right. There is no openness to revelation without risk but it is a condition of growth into maturity that we take that risk. The Church is called to act with as much prayer, discernment, listening and charity as possible, but there is no absolute guarantee that the Church will always get it right. What else could we expect? What else could a life that is free and valuable be like? Isn't scripture and the Church's tradition chock full of examples of people growing precisely through this risky, difficult process of change?

The key episode in the life of the early Church is the admission of the gentiles. It is hard for us to appreciate just how revolutionary this was. Gentiles could become part of God's people without becoming Jews. It was enough to recognize the Spirit at work in their lives. What seems obvious to us now was the cause of bitter division, slanging matches between apostles, doubt and compromise. There were those who wanted to uphold what had been received, because it was true and valuable. But in the end, the Church for the most part accepted that the Church was only being true to Christ and to the work of the Spirit if it was transformed into a more inclusive community.

Over time, that early openness was checked and indeed reversed. Alliances with imperial authority, the desire to defend its identity and discipline its members – these were the factors that led the Church into increasing reliance on hierarchy and measures of orthodoxy and obedience. The irony is that this 'traditional' Church which some still long for with nostalgia was simply the mirror image of the power structures of the surrounding world. Bishops became princes, the Pope an emperor. And even in the aftermath of the Reformation, pastors retained authority and control over the lives of the faithful, while co-operating readily with secular powers and markets.

No, the real counter-cultural Church is the communal witness to God's inclusivity in creation, in the work of Christ and in the freedom of the Spirit to blow where it will. The Church's structures and offices should reflect, however imperfectly, the nature of this God. No church office should be reserved for men alone, or for heterosexuals alone. Are they somehow made more in God's image than women or queers? Does Christ come first for men and then for women?

In some respects, these debates have already been won. Who could seriously argue that Christ should be represented only by white people? Or that those with disabilities should not be ordained? Despite the continuing prejudices that are as much part of the Church as any institution, an inclusive ethic is non-negotiable in many areas. Practice needs continually to be challenged and improved, but there is no credible move to turn back the clock. And this despite the fact that the scripture can be raided for as much if not more justification of racial segregation as it can for the submission of women, or the condemnation of homosexuals.

This should not surprise us. The Church is a living tradition, as scripture itself is. It is made up of a host of voices and experiences, and it changes through time. If we abandon the myth of the Church's original perfection, we should be able to find grace in this as well as threat or loss.

Grace, however, is never cheap. If the Church takes steps to make its offices and processes more transparent and inclusive, that will only underline the challenges it faces. Really to live as an inclusive community demands more than rules and procedures. It is a costly commitment to live with and along-side those who are not 'like us'. It is a difficult path of unlearning ingrained stereotypes and prejudiced habits of thought, and learning to be open to new voices, experiences and images of the divine. If Girard is right that we learn our desires by copying and competing with others, then a Christian community that seeks an alternative path of solidarity and forgiveness must truly be a searching and demanding place to take our stand.

The inclusive Church – as a process and a path rather than an assured result – never exists for itself alone. First and foremost, it exists because the grace of God calls it into being, and continues to do so even when it is broken and faithless. But this leads us to a further point: the Church exists to acknowledge the grace of God poured out on all humanity. This will cause it to celebrate the truth found in other expressions of faith and human value; to bear courageous witness to the ending of injustices which exclude people arbitrarily from fullness of life; and to offer itself in service to the world.

The 'how' of the Church thus takes precedence over the 'what' – the particular forms of ministry and structure which have evolved over time, sometimes through division and debate. These are important, and may each have gifts to offer the others. But we do not need to proclaim that one and only one type of church is the true blueprint for all others. A diversity of forms can foster the engaged and inclusive community we envisage.

This means, however, that we need to resist calls for a more centralized, authoritarian and uniform Church. Such a model may pander to our need for security, but it runs the risk of reducing the complex and mysterious reality of revelation to one-dimensional formulae to be parroted by a tightly defined in-group. In practice, it lends itself to a top-heavy hierarchical view, with little room for lay voices to be heard, and scant opportunity for risk-taking and development.

The Church therefore needs to live with a little messiness, a blurring of boundaries, as it seeks to follow one who was himself no respecter of boundaries, purity codes or religious insiders. If we accept this, is it still possible to speak of the general characteristics of the Church, or are we abandoned to endless fragmentation? In fact, of course, this tension is nothing new. The Church has always lived with difference and pluralism, both within and without its borders. But if we see it more as a living community of question, conversation and openness to transcendence than a monolithic guardian of unchanging absolutes, we can learn to find the Spirit in this situation. And we can start to find a richness in shared traditions which keeps the churches in dialogue with one another and the world.

With this in mind, it is worth looking again at those key elements of the Church's identity which have played such an important part in both church divisions and in recent conversations aimed at restoring its unity. What might an inclusive theological perspective have to say about baptism, Eucharist and ministry in the Church?

This might seem an odd question for a theology which seeks to engage with the world beyond the Church. Isn't much of that world – in the North at least – turning away from organized religion and its rituals to a more personal spirituality? This might be the case – but underlying this shift is a huge desire for connection, meaning, for a more holistic and liberating spiritual vision than that which seems to be associated with the churches. We believe we can learn from this, in common with many within the churches who are exploring alternative forms of worship, and take it as a cue to rediscovering a new and radical vitality in traditional symbols and rituals. They invite us beyond mere individualism and consumerism, into relationships and communities which are life-giving, creative and open to the gift of the Spirit. They put us in touch – literally – with the God who is in our midst, present in the most ordinary of things.

Life Poured Out: Baptism, Eucharist and Ministry in the Inclusive Church

Baptism has come to the fore as a touchstone of Christian identity in ecumenical discussions. It has enabled a greater degree of mutual acceptance and respect across denominational barriers. If we can at least recognize one another as baptized Christians, we have something solid on which to begin.

However, admirable as this position is, it risks becoming inward looking. As Christians huddle closer together, the price can be a turning away from our common, created human identity. The criteria for accepting people into baptism become more and more demanding, the hurdles become higher.

There is a strong argument in favour of this approach. After all, isn't baptism supposed to announce a radically changed way of life? The images associated with it – of death and new life, of cleansing and renewal – all point to a transformation of a person's life. Nevertheless, as we have maintained throughout, the mistake is to couple radical change and distinctiveness with an exclusive ideology of Christian belonging. In fact, when Christians become obsessed with their own difference from and superiority to the world outside, they are simply imitating the most mundane forms of human institution and community.

If the Church is to be about a different kind of belonging, baptism cannot simply be reduced to a means of plucking people out of the messiness and ambiguities of general human living. Baptism, at its root, means 'immersion', a phrase picked up by

Kierkegaard when he says we need to be immersed in the waters of existence. It is a dramatic act of journeying with Christ into all that water represented for ancient Israel: chaos, death, the uncontrollable, the ungraspable. The new life that we find there is not a fantasy of control and perfection, but a gift. Baptism connects us again with the original blessing and grace of creation, with the Spirit of God which broods over the waters in the first chapter of Genesis. It unites us with the people of Israel journeying away from the dehumanizing oppression of Egypt. It joins us with the inclusive Christ, who crosses boundaries of exclusion in order to bring the kingdom close.

Baptism, then, is not about joining a club, whose primary concern is to look after itself. Nor is it to be delivered into a problem-free life, or a belief structure of absolute certainty. It is a risky immersion into a life committed to breaking down barriers of exclusion, empowered by the grace-giving Spirit freely available to all in creation and renewed by Christ's invitation to share his death and new life.

In one specific sense, then, baptism is provisional, anticipating a fuller reality. A baptized person celebrates their full acceptance by the God of grace. But what baptism means can only ever be fulfilled when that acceptance is known by all. This is the 'not yet' – the dimension of future hope for a fully inclusive world – which structures all Christian living, and reminds us that we don't have God and God's promises within our controlling power. It is the world – indeed, all creation – that God in Christ comes to reconcile.

That is part of the sacramental nature of baptism. It is an action that goes beyond words, touching and enfolding us in ways that escape complete verbal definition. Sacraments open us to dimensions of truth which are more real and whole than any church pronouncement – and deeper and more challenging for that. The universal value placed on water helps to underline this. Water means life, cleansing, refreshment. If only we had faith in that gift of creation to make connections with people who come for baptism for themselves or their children, perhaps we would not be so anxious about trying to compel them to adopt the official line on Christian initiation.

The Eucharist affirms and nourishes this sacramental, baptismal faith. Whether you call it the Mass, the Lord's Supper, Holy Communion, or whatever, this sharing of bread and wine as the body and blood of Christ has been a central act of Christian worship from the very beginning. Its form and interpretation have of course changed over time, and it has been the focus for enormous controversy and division. The pity is that the Eucharist is the test of our hospitality, of our faithfulness to the radical hospitality of God in Christ. And when set against that standard, a fairly sorry situation is revealed, in which the Eucharist is tamed, domesticated, and made subservient to an agenda not its own.

Grand claims, but let us just touch on a couple of areas. First: the issue of insiders and outsiders. In some traditions, the Eucharist has become a rite reserved for those who already share a preconceived idea of fullness of faith. The recent furious debates in the Anglican Church have been peppered with threats to be 'out of communion' with opponents (even with one's own bishop). The implication is that in order to share communion we have to agree on a core body of doctrine and ethical attitudes. Recent reaffirmations of Catholic eucharistic discipline are based on the same point. And consider how the Anglican Church in particular has withheld communion from even its members until they are confirmed: until they have confessed in public an adult understanding of Christian doctrine and the meaning of communion itself. Baptism itself was somehow not a sufficient qualification to share the sacrament – a view that has only recently begun to be challenged.

All of this works by an inner logic: that only those who already share a pre-existing perfection of truth or moral purity can then go on to share communion. That reasoning works fine – until you question its starting point. Jesus, it seems, did not wait for those whom he touched, healed and ate with to confess to an elaborate body of doctrinal information. He ate with tax collectors and prostitutes – not *reformed* tax collectors and prostitutes. He even said they would enter the kingdom of God first (along, we read, with children, also considered 'nobodies' in Jesus' day). Note that he ate with those compromised by contact with foreigners, and with women. This at least should make us pause before buying into the view that the Eucharist is for those who are already signed-up members of the club.

It is worth noting that Jesus' table fellowship opened him to accusations of taint and impurity. It is arguable that it is these powerful taboos which are the real drivers for eucharistic exclusivity. We want to protect our borders, and keep out those contaminated with corrupt views and lifestyles. We want to eat with people like us, and we want to make sure the table is laid and administered by those whose hands are clean. Usually this means straight men, because they are assumed to be more spiritual, less chained to frightening bodily passions.

What a sanitized and anxious meal this has become! Perhaps the Eucharist has become so controversial precisely because it is an earthy, compromising act, a table where rich and poor, men and women, the normal and the weird could all partake. Controlling it therefore becomes a top priority for a religion driven by fear of impurity.

The second issue relevant here is that of spectacle. Because of fundamental developments in the understanding of the Church, the Eucharist became until relatively recently a spectator sport. Medieval developments resulted in a situation where the action of the mass was hidden behind screens, the priest standing with his back to the congregation, the faithful not even invited to share the bread and wine. Deeper changes underpinned this shift: the increasing emphasis on the holiness, defined as separateness, of the priestly class and of all they touched. It seems a far cry from the indifference to purity laws shown by Jesus and his disciples.

And what of the Protestant reaction to all this clerical excess and magical manipulation? That is a complex subject, but the tendency to stress word over sacrament had its own dangers. Rather than being a lived experience of the presence of Christ and the inbreaking of the kingdom, the Eucharist could become a memorial of a past event. And inclusion in that event could still be restricted to those who had grasped the 'text' of church teaching. Getting the Bible right comes first. Only then are we 'allowed' to share communion. It is all very cerebral and unforgiving.

As a spectator sport, the Eucharist falls prey to the besetting sins of the age: first, to turn religion into a ready-made object or teaching which we have to contemplate from afar or understand intellectually in order to be part of; and second, making communion into an essentially individualistic act between me and my God. To put it strongly, the Church was not shaped by Jesus' kingdom banquet. It administered it in the name of its own authority to control the life of the believer.

Part of the problem may be that the centrality of the Last Supper story can distort our perspective. It can suggest that this meal is essentially only for Jesus and the inner few, the 'real' followers. But what if the meal Jesus shared with his friends before he died is best understood in continuity with the meals he shared with many others through his ministry? Might we then escape, not only from the deeply patriarchal assumption that this is an event first and foremost for the male in-group, but also from the kind of theology which talks of the cross in isolation from all that Jesus said and did beforehand?

What if, for example, we started from another point: the parable of the wedding banquet? The story is found in Luke, Matthew and also in the Gospel of Thomas, each with differences. But in each case there is a reversal. Those invited to the banquet find reasons not to come. So the host sends out his servants to gather allcomers – the flotsam and jetsam of life, 'as many as you can find . . . both bad and good people' (Matthew 22:10) – into his feast. Just as striking as what this parable is suggesting about invitations and belonging is what it leaves out: there are no qualifications for a place at the table. As John Dominic Crossan observes:

> It is the random and open commensality of the parable's meal that is its most startling element. One could, in such a situation, have classes, sexes, ranks, and grades all mixed up together. The social challenge of such egalitarian commensality is the radical threat of the parable's vision.[1]

It is significant that the version of this parable in the Gospel of Thomas reaches an exclusive conclusion that is absent from the canonical Gospels. At the end of Thomas's version, Jesus sums up the meaning of the parable: 'Traders and merchants [shall] not [enter] the places of my Father.' Thomas (or a subsequent editor) turns the parable into a petty dig at business people. A comparison of Thomas's version with those of Matthew and Luke shows how the instincts of the canonical Gospel writers are inclusive.

It's worth developing further comments made earlier about

Jesus' table practice and his vision of a heavenly banquet. Jesus didn't just tell stories about food, he lived them. Jesus was branded a glutton and a drunkard, accused of eating with the compromised, the dirty and the sinful. And he did. That's the point. Jesus' opponents were right – according to the logic of a religion of purity, a religion of insiders. Jesus eats with Levi, Zacchaeus and a host of shady characters. He welcomes the touch of the morally dubious woman who anoints him in the house of the Pharisee.

Jesus proclaims a time of messianic abundance, when fasting is not necessary. In doing so, he calls to mind the visions of those who put together the book of Isaiah: in chapter 25, the promise of a feast of rich food prepared for all people, in the course of which death will be destroyed. And from a later part of the book, in chapter 55, the call to come and eat food and wine 'without price'. Doing away with the anxiety of death and undermining the economics of profit and loss, these meals offer political and psychological liberation to those who share in them. And this is without even mentioning the Passover meal, in which the angel of death flies by as God's people celebrate their freedom from slavery.

The Eucharist can have no less significance. It is a travesty to reduce it to a distant sacred mystery, or a confirmation of doctrinal correctness, or to spiritualize it so that it loses any anchoring in the world of blood, sweat and struggle. In Jesus' society, eating was a key indicator of belonging and status. In the way he ate, Jesus refused the boundaries of purity and status which eating was supposed to uphold. In so doing he challenged not only a religious establishment but also an entire empire.

The Roman empire shared in the ancient emphasis on honour and shame as the cornerstones of its value system. It took for granted the division between citizens and barbarians, free men and slaves. The Roman powers may have understood Jesus' claim to kingship in their own terms, but they were right to think that he was a threat. In the radicalism of the early Christian community, there were supposed to be no divisions in Christ, the wisdom and powers of the age were overthrown by all that the cross represented, military service and gladiatorial games were refused – the very lifeblood of empire.

The kingdom Jesus proclaimed was the exercise of God's active rule over everything. And the kingdom turned everything upside down: power, status, gender, purity, money: a whole empire's sense of itself was under attack.

And so it should be today. Whenever we celebrate the Eucharist, we should feel the foundations of this world and its empires tremble. We should catch the non-violent, recklessly inclusive life-pulse of Jesus' presence. We should be remade as an alternative community that is being liberated and shares in God's work of invitation. A spiritualized, apolitical, individualistic Eucharist will be happily tolerated by the new world order with its creed of market share secured by violence. A Eucharist which offers food without price could start a revolution.

Perhaps more important in this than how we understand and theologize about the Eucharist is how we do it, whether we can find the words, music, actions that connect faith with personal and social wholeness. Above all, we need to have the courage to offer an open table, to invite and welcome people to share communion without passing any tests, or belonging to any club. An open table is itself a sign of what the Eucharist is about: a new kind of belonging which can grow freely when we have jettisoned the baggage of authoritarianism, sectarianism and fear. For what is it that we are afraid of? That an unbeliever or an unreformed sinner might take the bread and wine? But don't we all doubt and fall? Can any of us say that we understand the mystery of God's gift of God's own self in this moment?

In the eyes of the empire, Jesus had no wisdom, no power, no honour and no shame. His kingdom, brought into being by his touching, healing, overturning and feasting, made that empire tremble. Christianity without Eucharist in this sense simply repeats the age-old religions: individual salvation as an escape from this world; submission to authority; insiders and outsiders. It turns God's dynamic rule into safe and stable structures. But Jesus does not just settle into the structures of the world as they are. He deliberately crosses boundaries, disturbs institutions, transforms situations. The cross and resurrection are in some ways only the most dramatic and radical instances of a life which refuses to be repressed and contained. Jesus is the kingdom in action, for all that we want to fix his essence in doctrines and structures. In the end, Jesus did not say 'believe this' or 'know this' or 'submit to this in memory of me'. He said '*do* this in memory of me'. And then he fed his friends.

Like baptism, Eucharist is both complete in its offer of life, and utterly provisional in its hope for a future yet to come. The feast set out on God's mountain for all people is an image of the Eucharist fulfilling its prophetic universalism. Every celebration looks to the coming of Christ, and to the time when the fruit of the vine will be drunk in the kingdom. In the meantime, the Eucharist becomes a missionary act: a joyous, compassionate, open table of hope for the world. It is a place where we can rediscover what it means to live out of the abundance of creation's gifts, without scarcity, fear and competitive desire distorting who we are called to be.

We have been discussing baptism and Eucharist, but it turns out that we have been talking about the ministry and mission and the Church all along. When the sacraments are freed from their church imprisonment, then they can help shape the Church for its service to the world.

In the light of all we have said so far, it will hardly come as a surprise to find that we continue to affirm a church ministry which is not arbitrarily restricted on grounds of race, gender, sexual orientation, disability or any of the other reasons human beings find to exclude one another. To those who claim that the Bible or church tradition upholds one or more of these exclusions, we offer this challenge: take seriously what we have said about the inclusiveness of creation's grace, of revelation and the incarnation of God in Christ. See how Christ gives and the Spirit sets free. And then ask: does any abstract theory of the Bible's literal truth or the infallibility of the Church really match up to what is on offer here? Don't those theories rather distort our humanity, setting up some as controllers of the truth? Don't they refuse the humility and humanity of how God has chosen to be revealed in the world?

Even if this point is accepted, however, we cannot rest there. It is not enough to take the Church as it is and simply open up its offices to all (good as that would be). We also need to look critically at whether those offices and structures truly reflect the nature of God. Do they exist to empower all God's people? Or are they self-serving, overly hierarchical and domineering? Do they serve the world and take the open invitation of God into the marketplace? Or are they about keeping the insiders happy? Do they encourage all to discover their vocation in life and work? Or are they more interested in restricting a sense of calling to the clergy alone?

As we have said earlier, we can provide no simplistic blueprint for how the Church should order its life. Different traditions will continue to do things differently. But each can rediscover the principles of inclusion at the core of its being. Not an added extra, but the heart of the gospel.

The Inclusive God

God Is Inclusive

This book started with a succinct thesis: 'The Church should be inclusive because God is inclusive.' The foregoing chapters have tried to show how God's inclusive nature is reflected in creation, in the person of Jesus Christ and in the Church. So far so good. But we also need to explore the inclusive nature of God as a topic in its own right.

One of the ways of thinking about God was to subject him to a logical analysis of his attributes. So God was said to be all-loving, all-powerful, all-knowing and so on. This approach was arguably valuable in so far as it enabled us to consider the idea of God from a variety of perspectives. But the analysis of God's attributes soon runs into trouble if it is taken to an extreme, because the separate attributes need to be reconciled with one another. And this isn't always easy.

God was said (by some at least) to be eternal and unchanging. As an unchanging being, God was deemed (as we have seen earlier) to be 'impassible', that's to say 'unmoved' by the vicissitudes of human history. So while God could be all-loving in a general sense, he could not, logically, be moved in time by any individual instance of human suffering. In this way, the attribute of impassibility imposed a restriction on the way God was allowed to exercise his love. God was also said to be 'simple',

that's to say composed of only one sort of substance. God's sim-
plicity was deduced from the belief that God must not contradict himself and that a God made of separate parts would be at
odds with himself. But if God is all-powerful, he can presumably
contradict himself, if he wants, or change his own nature. On
the other hand if God is unchanging, he can't change even if he
wants to. But if he can't change, this would mean that his power
is limited. And so on and so forth. The analysis of God through
his attributes soon gets itself twisted in knots, or stymied in logical contradictions such as: can God create a rock too heavy for
himself to lift?

Theologians have responded that all our knowledge of God
is imperfect and that contradictions are bound to arise when
a finite creature tries to get his mind around the infinite creator. Even so, when the method of considering God through his
attributes is allowed to turn God into a rational puzzle, it becomes religiously unsatisfying, and feels like the province of the
theological anoraks.

Underlying this approach is the presupposition that God
has various 'necessary' qualities – in other words, particular
attributes that God must possess in order to conform with our
idea of what God is like. God must be all-powerful, it is argued,
because it would be contradictory to think of a God with only
limited power. Similarly with the other attributes: God must be
simple, for example, because it would contradict our idea of God
to think of him as divided. This approach reached its apex in St
Anselm's famous 'ontological argument' which said that God
exists necessarily, because it would be contradictory to think of
the highest possible being as not existing. These arguments for
God's necessary existence and attributes resulted in a prescrip-
tive and exclusive theological mentality that locked God within
the cage of our preconceived ideas of what he *must* be like.

Inclusive theology works in a different way. When we say God is *inclusive* we are not suggesting another attribute to jostle with the others. The claim of inclusive theology is more fundamental, and interesting, than that. The inclusiveness of God refers to her nature, rather than to one of her characteristics. It's one thing to say God is 'all-loving', but something rather different to say 'God is love': the first statement posits an attribute, the second asserts identity. Love isn't something God possesses along with lots of other things – it's who she is. So with inclusion: God *is* inclusive.

God's inclusiveness cannot be approached by a merely theoretical process of enquiry. The inclusive God isn't an object of knowledge in any conventional sense. The exploration of the inclusiveness of God happens as lived experience: the experience on the one hand of living in the radically inclusive created order; and the experience on the other of trying to live out the gospel values of inclusion. A number of theologians now speak about theology as a kind of 'practice' or 'performance' or 'phronesis' (practical insight). In other words, theology is not a question of forming clear and distinct ideas about God in our minds; rather, we enact theology in the process of living the Christian life. This is what Jesus is getting at when he describes himself as 'the way, the truth and the life': theology is not merely theoretical, but a path that must be walked. We are back with Kierkegaard: 'Being a Christian is defined not by the "what" of Christianity but by the "how" of the Christian.'[1]

Theology is like life itself, and takes place as exploration and improvisation. The skills of the theologian are the capacity to keep theoretical insights firmly rooted in concrete experience, the ability to learn by trial and error, the acceptance of incompleteness and provisionality, an openness to new insights, an orientation towards the other, and the preparedness to engage in debate and conversation. These skills are required because the inclusive God is always being disclosed in the struggles and quests for the truly inclusive social order of God's kingdom. In life there is always some new stranger, or some new encounter from which our theology can learn. And at the end of life our theologies will lie unfinished just as life itself is an unfinished work. The search for the inclusive God is radically uncertain and open ended.

Kierkegaard concluded that a God who can accommodate the complexity of human existence must take the form of an absolute paradox, exemplified in the paradox of Jesus being both human and divine. The word 'paradox' not only means 'a contradiction' but, following its ancient Greek sense, something that goes against expectations, something that induces wonder and surprise. It is in this sense that St Luke uses the word *paradoxa* to describe the works of Jesus: 'amazement seized them all, and they glorified God and were filled with awe saying, "we have seen strange things (*paradoxa*) today"' (5:26).

The inclusive God is paradoxical in this sense: that he constantly confounds our prejudices, expectations and habitual patterns of thought. Creation is continually presenting us with new experiences, new relationships that challenge and overrun our exclusive and dogmatic ideas about him. The theologian who proceeds by clinging fiercely to a rigid view of what God must be like will either not find him or else find her cherished dogmas collapsing in her arms.

Beyond Idolatry: The Possibility of God

The inclusive theologian never has God as his possession, because God is always to be discovered in otherness and in conversation with other people. The inclusive God can never be used to justify violence or totalitarianism. Whatever we claim the inclusive God is, God is also something else as well. The Jewish philosopher Jacques Derrida sums it up well when he says: 'God sees from your side and from mine at once, as absolute third; and so *there* where he is not there, he is there; *there* where he is not there, is his place.'[2] The inclusive God represents a truth which is more complex – yes, more inclusive – than our narrow propositions can ever express.

In some ways the inclusive God sounds like the God of negative theology: we never say what he is, only what he is not. To be sure, inclusive theology draws upon the methods of negative theology in order to prevent our theological languages becoming idolatrous. In its very proper quest for a more exact way of speaking about God, theology can easily be tempted into offering ever more exclusive definitions, squeezing God into linguistic formulae of our own making. A negative theology corrects this tendency by insisting on the a priori inadequacy of all talk about God.

But the essence of inclusive theology is not, in fact, negative. The inclusive theologian is trying to say something positive about the complexity and incommensurability of God. But the incommensurable is impossible to describe and the task of evoking, expressing and naming the incommensurability of God can never have a conclusion. For purely practical reasons, the inclusive theologian is interested in the full range of possible discourses about God, rather than looking for one definitive theological language. It is in the interests of the inclusive theologian to explore unexpected theologies and to listen to the religious experiences and narratives of others. So 'the excluded' – whether excluded individuals, communities or cultures – are a resource for inclusive theology. Although the person who comes with a different theological perspective may unsettle us, this person is in fact a gift. The ability to recognize and honour this gift is part of the genius of the long tradition of inclusive theology.

The medieval theologian Nicholas of Cusa talks about God as '*possible* being' or 'actualized possibility' (for which he coins the term *possest*).[3] In other words, God is everything that it is possible for him to be. So the point of theology is to investigate God's possibilities. This means that inclusive theology is a positive discipline, because its essential task is not to say what God is not, but what *he may be*.[4]

This inclusive approach is radically different from the theologies of necessity which ask what God *must* be like. The investigation of God's necessary nature can easily become the insistence that God *must* fit our idea of him. In this way, theology moves from exploration to definition, from piety to idolatry. The result is a God that conforms at best to the limitations of our imagination, or at worst to our prejudices. By contrast, the inclusive theologian seeks to discover what is theologically possible, in the belief that the task of theology is to let God reveal his possible-actuality.

None of this will be very strange to Christians because the inclusive God is the God of scripture. The Old Testament lays a very firm theological foundation for the New by insisting that the face of God can never be seen and that we can never possess an 'adequate idea' of God. Yahweh is a law unto himself and he enforces his rights of divinity by consistently refusing to conform with Israel's expectations. Yahweh is contemptuous of the religious efforts of the Israelites and, through the prophets, takes the role of religious critic.

The Old Testament God resists all restrictive theological definitions, as Yahweh declares himself to be the god of his own possibility: 'I am who I will be . . . this is my name for ever, and thus

I am to be remembered throughout all generations' (Exodus 3:14–15). The ten commandments forbid the making of earthly images of God and this tradition of idoloclasm flows into the Jewish prophets: 'To whom will you liken God, or what likeness compare with him? The idol! . . . He who is impoverished (uncertain) chooses . . . to set up an image' (Isaiah 40:18). Belief in God is a process of being weaned from oppressive dependency on such limited reflections of our will to power and certainty. The idol is a thing in our grasp, however much we might surround it with an aura of supernatural mystique. Nicholas Lash therefore suggests that:

> Christianity is perhaps best seen as an educative project: as providing a context in which human beings may learn, however slowly, partially, imperfectly some freedom from the destructive bondage which the worship of any creature – however large or powerful, beautiful or terrifying, interesting or important – brings.[5]

This is why the New Testament is insistent that 'God is Spirit and that those who worship him, must worship in spirit and in truth' (John 4:24). If we harness John's idea of spirit to Paul's theology of 'spirit' as the anti-type of 'law', we can see how the New Testament tries to place God beyond the arm's length of our prescriptions and idolizations. The law seeks to define, the spirit seeks to express; the law is didactic, the spirit is exploratory. God, like the wind, is unconstrained: 'The wind blows where it wills, and you hear the sound of it, but you do not know whence it comes or whither it goes; so it is with everyone who is born of the Spirit' (John 3:18). The inclusive God is her own possibility.

The image of God as spirit is one in a cluster of biblical metaphors of instability and unrestricted movement: fire, water, organic growth (vines, trees, figs), light and life. The New Testament God is never portrayed as the rational platonic form that Augustine and his successors imagined. The inclusive God of the Bible is, rather, a living possibility which cannot be reduced to mere truth statements or authoritative narratives.

God in Relationship: The Trinity

One way in which Christianity has sought to preserve this truth is through the doctrine of the Trinity. That might sound an unlikely proposition, when we consider the bitter disputes and mutual accusations of heresy that accompanied the definition of the doctrine in the fourth and fifth centuries of the Christian era. Nowadays, despite enjoying a resurgence in academic theology, the Trinity is still regarded with puzzlement or indifference by many Christians (including preachers!).

This is a pity, because the Trinity is neither an intellectual puzzle understood only by specialists, nor a dry dogma we have to force ourselves to believe in, just because we're told it's good for us. No, the Trinity is an expression of the inclusiveness of God.

This is true on different levels. First, to speak of God as Trinity reminds us that there is never one and only one way of defining the divine. No catch-all dogma that we can come up with can ever say all that can be said. The reality of God is always richer, always more dynamic, mysterious and alive than our fumbling words and images can tell. Far from creating another dead formula, the doctrine of the Trinity always announces the incompleteness of any theological project we might care to construct. Experiencing our way into the heart of this mystery is a way of curing ourselves of the need for possessive, dominating, exclusive idols.

Secondly, the teaching affirms that God is not a lonely, static, cosmic dictator, or 'unmoved mover'. God is 'relationship without remainder', as Lash puts it.[6] In other words, God does not have a big divine ego she needs to protect. The most basic, creative, all-encompassing reality there can be is loving relationship. This is why, as we have seen, Christians affirm that God *is* love, not simply that God loves. And we make the further claim, that this inevitably entails that God is inclusive. God simply has no vested interest in consigning parts of humanity to damnation, or refusing to relate to people we consider impure or irreligious. How can it be that a God who *is* loving relationship rejects those of other faiths or none who express that love in their lives? How can it be that this Trinitarian God has no room for those who express their love in same-sex relationships? Why would this God refuse to be represented by half the human race on account of their gender?

This is not a charter for 'anything goes' or a sloppy abandonment of ethics. This love is the most searing and searching there can be – but one of the aspects of our life it brings into the light of judgement is our tendency to confuse right relationships with the cultural mores we have inherited. The Trinity teaches us that what matters is mutuality, honesty, commitment, openness, tenderness, justice. God is not defined by gender or sexual orientation, or race or even 'creed' in the narrow sense. If we force God to adopt our standards of judging others, we have to ask some serious questions about whether we are not placing our faith in idols of our own creation.

Thirdly, the revelation of the Trinity is shaped by the story out of which it arises: the story of Christians being caught up into the very life of God. God is not turned in upon himself.

Creation is neither an accident nor a necessity, but a free act of love. In creation, the God who is loving relationship opens herself to the risk of otherness, to granting being to a world that is not God, and to a humanity which so often rejects life-giving relationship. In Christ, God expresses in flesh her solidarity of love with that creation, and calls it from destructive exclusion to a new sort of community. In the Spirit, God empowers women and men to move beyond their self-imposed limits, to learn new languages in which to proclaim the primacy of love. And, just in case we think that we have got God's story all sewn up, the Christian tradition reminds us that we can't chop God up into bits and allocate separate roles to the three persons of the Trinity. At every moment, the whole reality of God touches our world. No wonder that the name of the Trinity is invoked at baptism and in blessings. From the beginning to the end, God is always being made known as the one who produces, nurtures, touches and inspires.

The teaching of the Trinity is therefore a charter for our own risk-taking openness to the world. It is an affirmation of the presence of God beyond all the boundaries we draw. It is a story of hope that all will be included and made whole by the God who is relationship without loss or remainder.

In the light of this argument, we should not be afraid of minting new metaphors for God. Many have already arisen from the struggles for inclusion in the Church, as different groups have made explicit their belief that they are made in God's image. God has been named as Mother, Lover, Friend, the Disabled God; Jesus has been encountered as the Black Messiah, the child of Sophia, as Christa the crucified woman. In a sense, this is simply a continuation of the way Christians have always drawn their images of God from their experience and surrounding culture. The difference is that these images are consciously adopted to reflect the liberating dynamic of God's loving relationship to all.

The only risk is that we allow ourselves to get talked into believing that, in order to follow this God, we have to reject our past. That would be a travesty. For one thing, many of these 'new' metaphors are in fact already there within the Christian tradition. More importantly, those who seek a more inclusive Church need to resist the temptation to romanticize being marginal, and have the confidence to reclaim the heart of Christian revelation and theology. There is much in the Church's past that needs criticism and correction. But we are still part of that story, however broken and sinful it has been, and learning to tell it in our own voices is part and parcel of the Spirit's work of reconciliation.

In particular, we should not be tempted to reject talk of the transcendence of God. For some, this talk is tainted by dualism, by a sense that God is made distant and disconnected from earthly life. They worry that this distant God stands behind many authoritarian and patriarchal practices. God is therefore virtually identified with an aspect of humanity, nature or culture.

Understandable as this move is, it is a failure of nerve. We hope that we have shown that holding to God's transcendence is in fact a liberating stance. It frees us from the idols of power and prejudice. It opens us to relationship with the Other, with a God who is never domesticated. And it therefore affirms our relationship to every 'other' as one that can be free, loving and life-giving.

The inclusive Church can only ever be a response to, a trust in, an enjoyment of the inclusive God. It is not a social arrangement designed to satisfy any other end. But in entering into the life of the Trinity, we find that this experience of gratuitous love always invites us into new relationships, hopes and struggles for a world more humane and whole. That exciting and dangerous invitation is the mission of those who have caught a glimpse of life-changing truth: God *is* love. God *is* inclusive.

Conclusion: Listening Theology

> The task is to become a Christian or to continue to be a
> Christian, and the most dangerous illusion of all is to become
> so sure of being one that all Christendom must be defended
> against the Turk – instead of defending the faith within one-
> self against the illusion about the Turk.[1]

Kierkegaard's words from the mid-nineteenth century have an
ominous prescience about them. For him and for us, theology
is no parlour game. In the world in which we live, it is a matter
of life and death. Do we want what is real to be defined by the
Christian fundamentalism which drives US imperialism? By
those who claim Islam, or Judaism or Hinduism, or any other
faith or ideology, as legitimation for conquest, violence and
ethnic cleansing?

Theology matters so much to us because, in one way or another, it underwrites ideas and passions which can work both
startling liberation *and* immense destruction. In this context,
to do theology out of defensiveness is the mirror image of the
world's anxieties, its craving for secure identities and closed
borders. We believe that Christianity should offer an alternative, one that will connect with the faith and virtue of many
beyond the churches. Renouncing anxious certainty, we might
find the grace to build communities of question, dialogue

and reconciliation. That is surely what the world needs of us now.

That is why we have laid so much stress on our claim that inclusive theology is rooted in what is real, and open to what is really possible. It is a concern for truth that drives us and calls us, though we know that there can never be an absolute and final way of stating the truth. That lust for certainty is part of the disease of which we need to be cured. The truth we seek is truth in relationship, a trust that commits us to a way of life.

It is worth recalling briefly that the New Testament concept of 'truth' was very different to our own. We now tend to think of 'truth' in empirical terms, seeing true statements as those which correspond in some way with 'facts'. The New Testament word for truth is *aletheia*, a complex Greek word meaning 'unforgetting'. This implies that the truth is somehow already embedded in human experience and needs to surface, or appear. It is not surprising that the existentialist philosopher Martin Heidegger should have been fascinated by this idea of truth, seeing it as an existential, rather than empirical, mode of truth. Religious truth surfaces in the process of living rather than existing 'out there' awaiting our descriptions. Jesus uses *aletheia* when he speaks of himself as 'the way, the truth and the life'. If we read the terms 'way' and 'life' as comments on the nature of 'truth' (which is at least one faithful reading) then 'truth' should be understood both as a path and a kind of existence. If *aletheia* is a living process in which the forgotten wisdom of existence surfaces through our struggles and experience, this implies that 'the truth' is more mysterious, and less predictable, than we might like.

The debates within the churches about inclusion issues are the symptoms of a wider malaise: our inability to come to terms with the anxieties that surround human life, sharpened by the fast-changing nature of modernity. But 'perfect love casts out fear' (1 John 4:18), and the Christian journey is one of letting go of all false securities to embrace a deeper freedom, a childlike maturity.

This book is intended only as a small contribution to that journey. We are aware of how inevitably limited it is, and how much it leaves unsaid. Nevertheless, it represents a challenge and an invitation which we believe is important and timely. It is a claim that Christian theology is inclusive at its heart, not just on the edges, or because of some fashionable reinterpretation. Those of us who believe in this vision are here to stay. This is our (broken) home.

It is also a call to do theology in a way that is not self-enclosed, but open to other voices, disciplines and realities. There is so much that demands exploration, from globalization to genetics, from cyberspace to climate change. New forms of identity, relationship and community are being forged, and we need to ask how mutuality and inclusion can be embodied in these strange and evolving contexts.

Theology can have much to say to the world if recovers its self-confidence while abandoning delusions that it can lord it over all other discourses. The way of the theologian must echo the Christian way of prophetic service. Indeed, we affirm that all Christians *are* theologians. It is the way we live the faith that gives it substance, and embodies what we believe. That process of becoming a Christian should be characterized by hospitality to the stranger and the recognition of God's image in every neighbour. Theology is part of a life lived in the free Spirit, not a rulebook for the Christian ghetto.

We do not live from ourselves, but from God. We do not live for ourselves, but for the world God is creating. The inclusive Church is a missionary Church because the gifts of God cannot be grasped by ourselves alone. It is important to end on this outward-looking note. Mission can no longer be valid as a form of colonialism, patronizing or demonizing the other faiths and cultures it encounters. But the mission of God – and therefore of the Church – is something very different. It is a bearing witness in mind and heart, flesh and blood, to a commonwealth of grace. It is written in the lives of those who spoke from the margins, to claim their God-given humanity.

Mission now demands that we become listeners, like the suffering servant who says of God, 'morning by morning he wakens – wakens my ear to listen as those who are taught' (Isaiah 50:4). To be attentive to what God is creating, where God is sending us, we need to be aware of God's presence in the world around us, and especially in the lives of those ignored or vilified by the powers that be. Making connections between the struggles and passions and dreams of our world, the missionary Church can be a bridge-builder, a community of participation and an advocate for change. This is not passivity. A listening Church can be truly transformative, because it works with the grain of God's inclusive Spirit, resisting the temptation to drop its cherished insights like bombs from a clear blue sky. It discovers the stuff of truth in the warp and weft of lived reality. And sometimes – often – it can be surprised into a new insight.

This attitude of listening, openness and responsiveness does not arise because the inclusive theologian has no ideas of her own, or because she is without convictions, still less because her convictions are not held with passion. In the very act of listening the inclusive theologian is affirming her conviction in the inclusive God. Listening is theological action.

We live in a world that is continually failing to listen to the voices of the poor and the outsider. In this context, listening is a distinctive act of prophecy and witness. The opposite of listening is not speech. Listening is in fact *a form of speech*, a way of speaking the word 'inclusion'. Listening is a 'speech act' that affirms the one listened to. The opposite of listening is not-listening and ignorance. This is not to say that we must agree with all that we hear, or that we should not confront, dispute and negotiate. Listening is part of conversation, indeed it is the precondition of meaningful conversation. Without listening, theology degenerates into rhetoric.

Listening also presumes that our speech about God is imperfect and incomplete. Our theology is spoken within fluid cultural and linguistic contexts. The senses and meanings of language are not static, so our narratives must continually be retold and our theologies must be rewritten. There is no final theological language, no ultimate theological book. The work of the theologian can never be finished. Theology is always subject to re-narration, translation and reinterpretation, so the inclusive Church listens because it *must*. The person who listens acknowledges that she is still in search of an adequate theological language, that she is always still learning how to speak as a theologian.

Why? Because we believe the gospel is truth, a truth that is in the process of being unforgotten and disclosed. We believe the open-armed Christ is the Way, the Truth and the Life. We believe in an Inclusive God. The response to such a God should not be the homage of a sect, speaking from the towers of its citadel. The response to the inclusive God must be an inclusive Church immersed in, and committed to, the reality of God's creation.

Notes

Introduction

1 John Milbank, *Theology and Social Theory*, Oxford, Blackwell, 1990, pp. 387-8.
2 Milbank, *Theology*, pp. 387-8.
3 John Robinson, *The Honest to God Debate*, ed. J. Robinson and D. Edwards, London, SCM Press, 1963, p. 229.
4 Paul Tillich, *The Eternal Now*, London, SCM, 1963, p. 94.
5 Tillich, *The Eternal Now*, p. 94.
6 David Tracy, *The Analogical Imagination*, New York, Crossroad, 1981, p. 113 .

1 Creation

1 Augustine, *Confessions*, XIII, 2.

3 Jesus and the Kingdom

1 John Dominic Crossan, *The Historical Jesus*, New York, HarperCollins, 1992, p. 422.
2 The Essene War Scroll (1 QM VII, 4–5).
3 Ched Myers, *Binding the Strong Man: A Political Reading of Mark's Story of Jesus*, Maryknoll, New York, Orbis, 1988.

6 The Inclusive Church

1 Crossan, *The Historical Jesus*, p. 262.

7 The Inclusive God

1 Søren Kierkegaard, *Concluding Unscientific Postscript*, ed. H. and E. Hong, Princeton, Princeton University Press, 1992, p. 610.
2 Jacques Derrida, *A Taste for the Secret*, Oxford, Polity Press, p. 71.
3 'Trialogus de Possest' in (tr. Jasper Hopkins) *A Concise Introduction to Nicholas of Cusa*, Minneapolis, Minneapolis University Press, 1980, pp. 62–153.
4 For a fascinating exploration of this idea see Richard Kearney, *The God Who May Be: A Hermeneutics of Religion*, Bloomington, Indiana University Press, 2001.
5 Nicholas Lash, *Believing Three Ways in One God*, London, SCM, 1992, p. 21.
6 Lash, *Believing Three Ways*, p. 32.

Conclusion: Listening Theology

1 Kierkegaard, *Concluding Unscientific Postscript*, p. 608.

Index